Eric Hobsbawm was born in Alexandria in 1917 and educated in Vienna, Berlin, London and Cambridge. A fellow of the British Academy and the American Academy of Arts and Sciences, with honorary degrees from universities in several countries, he taught until retirement at Birkbeck College, University of London, and since then at the New York School for Social Research in New York. In addition to *The Age of Revolution 1789–1848*, *The Age of Capital 1848–1875*, *The Age of Empire 1875–1914* and *Age of Extremes: The Short Twentieth Century 1914–1991*, his books include *Revolutionaries*, *On History*, *Bandits* and *Uncommon People*.

Other titles by Eric Hobsbawm

Non-fiction
*The Age of Revolution 1789–1848*
*The Age of Capital 1848–1875*
*The Age of Empire 1875–1914*
*Age of Extremes: The Short Twentieth Century 1914–1991*

Essays
*On History*
*Revolutionaries*
*Uncommon People*

# THE NEW CENTURY

---

ERIC HOBSBAWM

In conversation with
Antonio Polito

Translated from the Italian by
Allan Cameron

An *Abacus* Book

First published in Great Britain by Little, Brown and Company in 2000
This edition published by Abacus in 2000

Copyright © Gius. Laterza & Figli SpA, 1999
Translation © Editori Laterza 2000

This translation of *Inervista sul nuovo secolo*
is published by arrangement with Gius. Laterza & Figli SpA, Roma-Bari.

A CIP catalogue for this book is available
from the British Library.

ISBN 0 349 11336 X

Printed and bound in Great Britain by
Clays Ltd, St Ives plc

Abacus
A Division of
Little, Brown and Company (UK)
Brettenham House
Lancaster Place
London WC2E 7EN

# Contents

# THE NEW
# CENTURY

———

# Introduction

I**T IS PART OF LIFE** and business to question ourselves about where the future is leading. Where possible, we all make an attempt at it. However, predicting the future must necessarily be based on knowledge of the past. Future events must have some connection with past events, and this is where historians come in. They are not in the pursuit of profit, in the sense that they are not exploiting their knowledge to secure earnings. Historians can attempt to uncover those elements of the past which are important, and identify the trends and the problems. Thus we must try to make predictions, albeit with certain reservations. We have to be aware of the danger of aping the fortune-teller. We need to understand that, in practice and in principle, much of the future is entirely unpredictable. Nevertheless, I believe that it is single, specific events which are unpredictable, while the real problem for historians is to understand how important they are or could be. Sometimes analysis can show them to be significant, other times not.

For example, it is not important for an insurance company to know whether this house in which we are sitting and talking will burn down to the ground next week. All insurers need to know in order to carry out their business profitably is the general probability of house fires. On the other hand, it is obviously much more important for me as the owner of this house to know whether it will catch fire in the next few days. Again, if twenty young women and twenty young men went camping in the summer, there would be a high probability of relationships being formed. The important thing for those young people would be to know who would go off with whom. But for the historian or social scientist, this would be completely irrelevant. What counts is the probability of it occurring. Sometimes events have no importance for the historian for the purpose of prediction, and sometimes they do, and do so quite spectacularly. These are the limits on prediction.

So what we can do in this conversation is to discuss problems as they appear today, and identify some probabilities. Sometimes these probabilities will be very high, while at other times they could be thrown into disarray by completely unpredictable events. Take the bombing of the Chinese Embassy in Belgrade, which is certainly historically significant, even though we do not yet know how significant, but it is equally certain that it was not at all predictable.

*You are famous for having defined the twentieth century as the "Short Century," which started late in 1914 with the First World War and ended in advance in 1991 with the collapse of the Soviet Union. If your periodization is correct, we have already been living in the new century for a decade. Do we have enough material to attempt to sketch it out? Are the distinctive features of the new era already identifiable, or are we still in a transitional phase with uncertain results?*

I made a choice by identifying 1991 as the end of the Short Century (in a way, it was easier to set the beginning in 1914), but this was not the only possibility when I wrote my book in 1994. I chose that date for reasons of expediency. Exact dates are always matters of historical, didactic, or journalistic expediency. Take, for example, the war in Kosovo. It is certainly possible to identify the starting date as the first night of NATO bombings, yet we know that the Kosovo crisis went back over many years. In 1992, we already knew that it was going to become serious and would affect the interests of the United States. Washington officially notified Yugoslavia of these interests, and to make it even clearer, it sent troops to Macedonia. Then everything was overshadowed by the Bosnian crisis. But again, with the end of that crisis, we could then fix the date of the war's beginning with the commencement of the Serbian "ethnic cleansing" and the outbreak of the armed revolt by the Kosovo Liberation Army.

In other words, singling out a particular date is a convention and not something that historians are ready to fight for. There is only one clear indicator for the end of the end of the Short Century: we know that since 1973 the world economy has entered a new phase. And if you believe, as I still do, in Kondratev's theory of long waves, that period was destined to end some time in the nineties, but exactly when is not so clear. I thought that at the beginning of the decade the collapse of the Soviet Union, which coincided with a serious crisis, a depression in the economy of the Western countries, constituted a reasonable date for the change of an era. Clearly, however, it could also have been the subsequent economic crisis of 1997–98, which marked the end of the century. It is only possible to know when a period ended when that period has ended for a considerable period of time.

For example, it could be said that between 1945 and the early 1970s, the world economy underwent relatively minor fluctuations, while since 1973, we have again found ourselves in a period marked by very powerful jolts: the crises of

1980—82, 1990—91, and 1997—98. It is possible that a similar trend is in store for us in the future, making it difficult to establish a precise date for the transition from one era to the next. It is also clear that the effects of the collapse of the Soviet Union have proved to be serious and lasting. I believed and wrote that it was going to be a very significant problem, but I also underestimated its gravity. If I were to rewrite *The Age of Extremes* today, I would be more cautious in predicting a sudden worldwide expansion of the capitalist economy in the near future. As a result of the collapse of the Soviet Union, this development could be delayed even further than I predicted in my book. All this makes it very difficult to know whether we have yet emerged from the "short" twentieth century.

In spite of this, I think we already know something about what the new era will be like because some of its political and economic features are already clear. In many ways, we can undoubtedly claim to be already living in the new century. In terms of international politics and of ideologies, it is quite clear that the demise of the communist regimes in the East has constituted a real historical break, and today's world is dominated by the effects of those events. Thus we can attempt to say something about this new era.

*Where does this belief in history come from, this ambition to be able to read the future predicted from the past?*

I was attracted to history, in the first place, by reading Karl Marx. I mean that Marx gave me the awareness that it is an instrument without which we cannot understand what is happening in the world. I was persuaded by his idea that history can be seen and analyzed as a whole, and it has . . .

I wouldn't say laws because that is too reminiscent of old-style positivism; it has a structure and a pattern, which are human society's story of evolution over a long period of time.

I have to say that in my youth our teachers were not interested in this type of history. But I started to study this discipline, proved to be reasonably good at it, and so I embraced it. I could also have studied sociology or anthropology, subjects which are equally related to the evolution of societies. I think I learned a lot from Michael Postan, a teacher at Cambridge who had emigrated from Eastern Europe, because he was the only one who knew something about the debate on the Continent and the continental European literature, and was aware of the teachings of people like Marx or the Russian sociologists and historians. Of course, being a Russian emigré, he was fiercely anticommunist. But he knew his stuff. In the ten years which followed the war, our generation learned its history in regular seminars held by historian friends and members of the Communist Party of Great Britain, the so-called Communist Historian Group: Christopher Hill, Maurice Dobb, E. P. Thompson, the medievalist Rodney Hilton, myself, and others. Also after the war, there was a debate with historians, many of them French, from other countries. I had a lot of sympathy for the Annales School, with one difference, however. They believed in a history that never changes, in the permanent structures of history, while I, on the other hand, believe in history that changes.

*You have never ceased to acknowledge your debt to Marx. What ultimately does the Marxist interpretation consist of?*

Above all, a Marxist interpretation suggests that, in having understood that a particular historical stage is not permanent, human society is a successful structure because it is capable of change, and thus the present is not its point of arrival. Second, one can study the modus operandi, the ways in which a particular social system functions, and why it generates or fails to generate the forces of change. For example, in order to analyze the Chinese economy over a period of centuries, you need to understand what it was in that country which prevented and impeded change, which stabilized rather than destabilized that society, in spite of so many elements of economic and technological progress. While in the West, the problem is to understand exactly the opposite. That is why the history which interests me is analytical; that is to say, history attempts to analyze what happened rather than just uncovering it. I don't mean that it can be used to understand exactly why the world developed in a certain manner, but it can tell us how various elements coming together within a society serve to create an historical dynamic, or conversely, fail to cause it.

# 1) War and Peace

*The twentieth century has ended with a war, just as the Short Century started with the catastrophe of the Great War. As though time had not moved on, the national question has exploded again and put the great powers to the test. So is history repeating itself? How did we move from the end of the Cold War to the return of "hot war?" How is it possible that there are more refugees now than at the end of the Second World War?*

It is true that in some ways the war in the Balkans has been truly a war with all the hallmarks of a bygone era. It is the continuation of the Balkan wars and more generally of the wars produced by the international system of powers in the twentieth century, and before that, in the nineteenth. The Balkan War is, if you like, the final consequence, the last by-product of the Great War. That conflict saw the collapse of the prebourgeois, multinational empires. The end of the Hapsburgs and the Ottomans produced the nationalist map of Southeast Europe, while the October Revolution preserved the unity of what had been the empire of the tsar. Now that that regime has also collapsed, we are witnessing similar consequences in that part of the world.

I think that it is more important to analyze the manner in which the general nature of war and peace has changed at

7

the end of the twentieth century. The general nature of war is a much more significant problem than its specific reasons. It is, for example, more important than asking ourselves whether or not Kosovo was a just war which clearly appeared as an enormous and urgent problem while the war was raging in the spring of 1999. But for future historians who will study the war, other questions will seem a great deal more interesting, because they define the distinctive features of this fin de siècle and say something about the coming century.

The thing that most interests me is how war has changed, both in the political and technological sense. Is it still possible to have a war between the great world powers? The answer is no, as long as America is the only superpower. It is possible that, sooner or later, China will reach a military capability to rival effectively the USA. I don't want to say whether this will happen or not. But what does seem certain is that a new world war is not probable until this happens.

Second, is a nuclear war possible? On the one hand, the unlikelihood of a world war makes nuclear war improbable. However, the use of nuclear arms in a war is, in my opinion, possible and not improbable, because technology has steadily increased their availability, made them more widely producible and more rapidly transportable. Hence the exclusion of the risk of a world war does not eliminate the risk of wars in which nuclear arms could be used.

Third, are the more conventional wars between states, to which we have been accustomed, still possible? The answer is that they never ceased, except in the areas where the two great superpowers confronted each other directly and therefore were very careful to avoid the risk of a nuclear catastrophe. We have had conflicts in South Asia between India and Pakistan, and there have been wars in the Middle East be-

tween Iran and Iraq. So wars even continued during the period of the nuclear nightmare. The possibility of more wars
is therefore high. There are certain regions of the world
where this is extremely improbable. We tend to forget that
there are regions, like Latin America, where no army ever
crossed the border of an enemy state throughout the twentieth century, with the one exception of the Chaco War between Bolivia and Paraguay (1932–35). There have been an
abundance of massacres and civil wars, but not wars between states. We do not know to what extent this will also be
true of Europe in the twenty-first century. In any event, this
kind of war cannot be ruled out in the future world, although they will perhaps not be as important as they were in
the twentieth century.

I believe that what is new about the situation in the Balkans is that the line which distinguishes internal conflicts
from international conflicts has disappeared or is tending to
disappear. This means that the difference between war and
peace, and between the state of war and the state of peace
has also diminished. The Yugoslav situation is a typical example. Although it arises from an antagonism, which the
Serbs consider to be an internal question, there has also been
an external intervention. This is something which, in the
nineteenth century and up to the end of the Cold War, would
have been completely impossible: foreign armies which
cross borders to resolve an internal conflict within a sovereign state. In this case, one of the two parties to the conflict
even refused to acknowledge that a war was taking place. It
seems impossible to deny that bombing another state constitutes an act of war. Yet, officially, war was not declared,
and therefore some people argue that a state of war did not
exist. This is the staggering novelty of the situation.

Clearly, we are dealing with a consequence of the end of

the Cold War. During that period, the relative stability of the world was essentially based on the golden rule of the international system: no one crosses the borders of another sovereign state, because the result would be to upset the balance. Since the end of the Cold War, we have seen the end of this self-limitation. Central Africa, Yugoslavia, Kosovo, Iraq: it is not at all clear whether these were wars or not. The very fact that there was a great deal of debate about whether they were just or unjust was another way of expressing our perplexity, faced with a completely new phenomenon. The Italian philosopher Bobbio was being fairly logical in saying that he doesn't even want to pose this question, because the real question is whether the war in Kosovo was legal in accordance with the past rules. The answer is no. The old rules of war and peace, which distinguished between internal conflicts and international ones, have been eroded, and it does not appear at all probable that they will be restored in the near future.

There are also differences in the way in which war is fought, enormous differences. Some were predictable, other less so. The first is the transformation of war brought about by advanced technology. Initially, we feared that it would bring about conflicts that were more bloody and devastating. But, since the Gulf War, we have known that advanced technology produces a much more precise and discriminating power of destruction. Intelligent bombs are capable of selecting particular objectives and avoiding others. Leaving aside operational incidents and the risks of "friendly fire," this new reality is important, because it restores the distinction between combatants and noncombatants, which had disappeared in the twentieth century when wars were increasingly directed against civilians. This allowed NATO to say in the Kosovo War, for example, we are not targeting

civilians, but only troops and their installations, at leas
principle.

On the other hand, this makes possible an increasingly
frequent and frivolous recourse to destruction. If you believe
yourself to be so powerful that you can choose exactly what
you want to destroy, it becomes easier to be tempted to resolve your problems by bombing, as occurred in Iraq. In this
sense, advanced technology increases the risks of armed conflicts, at least by the nations that have it at their disposal.
Moreover, it underestimates the risks of what is called "collateral damage." I do not mean the people killed by mistake,
but the enormous damage caused to infrastructures by
which a community lives and produces. Given that there
isn't the risk of killing too many human beings, you might
think that this is a very civilized way of conducting a war.
However, there are estimates that the Serbian economy suffered greater destruction in a few weeks than it suffered
throughout the whole of the Second World War. The effects
do not only concern the Serbian economy: the destruction of
the bridges over the Danube, for example, has seriously
damaged the economy of the entire region, which extends
from southern Germany to the Black Sea and beyond.

Finally, an enormous difference has been created at a
lower level, that of the peoples who do not have access to
advanced technology, between the war conducted by aircraft at fifteen thousand feet with highly sophisticated
bombs, and the war on the ground, where people physically
kill other people, perhaps with machetes or knives, as occurred in Central Africa. This was particularly evident in
Kosovo, where the two different wars progressed simulta-
neously without contacts between each other. In the past,
"guerrillas" were armed with rifles and machine guns; now

they have rocket launchers and portable antiaircraft weapons. This is another product of the Cold War, which flooded the world with its capacity for producing arms. While there were no actual wars between the powers in that period, the armaments industry was working at full capacity, as though a general mobilization was in operation. Obviously, the end of the Cold War immediately made this vast arsenal available. I will give you an example: the conclusion of the civil war in El Salvador suddenly put enormous quantities of automatic rifles on the market. They could be bought on the border for a hundred dollars each, and then carried to Colombia for resale at five hundred dollars. It was a good business for some people. Now the world is full of arms, and this creates a new situation in which "freelance" armed groups appear. They are not necessarily linked to a government, but they are ready for war.

I see this as another sign of change: the relationship which is emerging and connects wars between states or organized movements to private wars between private individuals or organizations. Potentially, it is a fundamental change. During the century that is now coming to an end, it has been assumed, with a few exceptions, that armed conflicts were conducted between states or by quasi-state organizations (resistance movements in Italy or Yugoslavia, the African National Congress, and movements of national liberation). They were not organized by private enterprises, as occurred in Italy during the age of *condottieri*, or by leaders of mercenary armies. Up to the seventeenth century, European states would hire armies. In the Thirty Years' War, Wallenstein was the last entrepreneur who hired out his army to the states in conflict.

Today, we have a return to private enterprise in war. This is very clear in parts of the world where states are disintegrating, as in Africa, and where mercenary bands are used sometimes by warring factions and sometimes by governments.

On top of this, you need to add recent trends concerning wars directly linked to governments, such as the tendency to abolish general conscription even in countries which until now have based their army on national service. The general trend is to concentrate on the use of professional and highly qualified military personnel. Without doubt, this process creates room for private enterprise. Even in the most advanced countries, there is now a gray area where highly specialized military personnel and private businesses which provide security services are working together. In Great Britain, soldiers from SAS commando units obtain similar jobs on retirement with companies that provide consultancy and operational services to governments in relation to warfare and antiterrorism.

There is already a mass of studies into the prospects for private armed forces in future wars; for instance, by the Institute of Strategic Studies in London. Some think that the prospects aren't great, particularly because such services are not reliable. But, on the other hand, we have noticed in the case of the Gulf War a widespread use of private enterprise for logistical support in warfare. This was a little like what happened in the civilian field during the Thatcher period, when services previously provided by the government were put out to outside tender. I believe that munitions, provisions, and clothing for the troops will be increasingly tendered to private firms.

*As in Macedonia, where an American company follows the NATO troops and provides logistical support.*

Exactly. This is a new phenomenon in relation to the twentieth century. It is typical of a new era. It arises from the relative disintegration of the state power in some parts of the world. It has resurrected the figure of the "warlord," who has not existed in Europe since the fifteenth and sixteenth centuries. These people were capable of influencing political events because they had organized their own private armies. It reminds me of the situation in China for the fifty years between the collapse of the empire and the revolution, when there was no effective government, only the power guaranteed by the armies of the warlords. Some were ex-bandits, like Chan Tso Lin, who ruled Manchuria and transformed himself into a general. I feel that the current situation, a mixture of private warfare and wars between states, means this phenomenon will again be probable in areas where the state is disintegrating markedly.

This is reinforced by another new factor: the extraordinary wealth that is now available to private entities. Today, it is possible for individuals or corporations to possess as much money as states. This is partly due to the growth of illegal businesses such as drug trafficking and smuggling. As far as I know, not a single government has financed the Kosovo Liberation Army, partly because I believe that the last thing that Western governments wanted is the creation of an independent Kosovo. Equally, I do not believe that the Albanian government has assisted them significantly, because it is not in a position to grant financial aid to anyone. Therefore, the KLA is almost certainly being funded by the illegal trafficking run by the Kosovar and Albanian mafia, as happened in Chechnya. I am not saying that this is money spent on an unjust cause, but I want to say that groups which otherwise would not have had political significance have acquired it by resorting to resources which were not available

in the past. This is particularly evident in Colombia, w.
the government has practically lost control of large area.
the country, because the groups which dominate them are
sufficiently well financed to fight and to resist. There is really no lack of resources in the world at the moment.

In my opinion, these features will become increasingly
important in future wars. It is very easy for three hundred
well-armed militiamen, theoretically not controlled by any
state or government, to range over vast areas plundering and
cleansing them of "enemies." As we have seen in Kosovo,
you do not need many men to burn houses and villages, and
put their inhabitants to flight. The less armed conflicts are
structured and state-governed, the more dangerous they become for the civilian populations, hence the exceptionally
high number of refugees in the world today.

I know someone who has worked for some years with the
United Nations in Sudan, a country tormented by a long
civil war. She told me that initially they had to apply to the
leaders of the liberation movement to have humanitarian
access to areas in the south. But in due course, the territory
they controlled broke up into a series of principalities governed by individual generals, who also became masters of
the refugees' fate, and the UN now had to negotiate with
each of them to be able to help the refugees.

*It is just as well then that we have television to show us the
suffering of refugees.*

There can be no doubt that the new role of public opinion
has had a decisive role in changing the nature of war. The
"CNN effect," as we might define it. Selective news of what

is happening becomes immediately available. This is another result of the end of the Cold War, because government control and censorship of information is much less than in the past, and on occasions even impossible. This was not the case during the Vietnam War, and still less during the years immediately after it. Television's extraordinary domination has made it impossible now for governments to manage international crises in the manner they were accustomed to. But it is also an instrument at their disposal for mobilizing public opinion with a rapidity unthinkable in the past. Consider the amount of time required to transform either the sinking of the *Lusitania* or the Tonkin Gulf incident into a casus belli. The effect of television is immediate, but it is also no longer controllable.

This can be seen in the way in which both Saddam and Milosevic allowed television teams from the countries they were at war with to stay and film what they wanted to show to Western public opinion, while in the past the natural reaction would have been to black out the screens in a traditional Stalinist manner. This has important effects on the politics of war.

*You have described the new characteristics which war tends to adopt at the end of the Short Century. However, these include the arrival on the scene of the concept of the "just war" and the "unjust war." Is it just, in your opinion, that democracies wage war against dictators in the name of Universal Human Rights?*

I am a little skeptical about this. It doesn't appear to me that governments go to war because it is either just or unjust. Of course, they tend to justify them, in order to gather public support, by claiming that they are just. It is extremely important to convince public opinion. It is decisive to present the war in such a manner that people perceive it as legitimate and just. But it is very difficult to find historical examples of governments which went to war over something other than national interests.

Obviously, there are exceptions. One of these is constituted by revolutionary regimes, that is, expressions of a revolution, which sometimes wage war for other reasons based on morality, ideology, or national liberation. But even these regimes, as soon as they have stabilized, adopt foreign policies typical of states and start to act on the basis of national interests.

On this point, we must always remember that the United States of America is, to some extent, an ideological power which originated, just like the Soviet Union, from a revolution, and therefore feels the need to guide the world in accordance with its principles, as an essential part of its foreign policy.

This can be very dangerous. I have no doubt that the United States would like to change the world, and that the protection of human rights is part of its ambition. In spite of this, I cannot think of one time when the USA went to war exclusively to do good, without any significant national interests being involved.

Today, there undoubtedly is a genuine debate about the importance of human rights in order to ascertain to what extent their defense could be guaranteed by the use of military force. But I am still of the conviction that neither NATO nor the United States thought seriously about going to war entirely on grounds of principle and ethics. Not even the Second World War was fought for this principle. Of course, the Allies were on the right side and their victory saved the world from Nazism, but the European democracies and the Soviet Union were dragged into it by Hitler, and the United States by Japan.

*You experienced anti-Semitism in Germany, because of your Jewish origin. For you, January 30, 1933 was not only the date on which Hitler became chancellor of the Reichstag, because you also remember it as "a winter afternoon in Berlin, when at the age of fifteen [you] were returning home to Halensee with [your] younger sister from the school at Wilmersdorf, and somewhere along the road [you] saw a newspaper headline. [You] can still read it, almost as though it was a dream." Do you also feel, like Elie Wiesel, that you need to halt ethnic hatred even with force, before it can strike home? Do you believe that Milosevic's "ethnic cleansing" constitutes the crime of genocide, and is it comparable to the Holocaust?*

I think not. "Genocide" has become an overused term, and has therefore lost some of its meaning, a little like what happened to the word "fascism." Genocide is a plan to eliminate an entire ethnic group. In a way, it is a logical and extreme extension of ethnic cleansing. For example, information has now emerged which suggests that ethnic cleansing in Srebrenica came close to genocide. Nevertheless, there is a fundamental difference between driving people away from their land, telling them "off you go somewhere else," and implementing their total elimination. The Nazis killed Jewish men, women, and children. What happened with ethnic cleansing was the deportation of women, old men, and children, and the selection of men of fighting age for imprisonment and physical elimination. This does not in any sense diminish the moral gravity of ethnic cleansing, but I believe we must be able to make that analytical distinction. Ethnic cleansing is a phenomenon that occurs with various degrees of gravity, and can be pushed to the limits of genocide. It is so vile in itself that it does not need to be made worse by identifying it with genocide. The fact is that, although no one likes to discuss this in public, generals and politicians do not hesitate to assert in private that in history ethnic cleansing has often helped to simplify problems. This is another reason that makes me skeptical about the moral motivations of the war in Kosovo. If the Germans had not been driven from Slovenia, would that country be the quiet and peaceful place we know today? In the end, the conflict in Bosnia was ended by separating the different populations which lived in different parts of the country. Personally, I think it is mistaken to allow it to happen, even just as a matter of principle. It should not even be discussed as a theoretical or possible solution. But we live in a very violent world, and it happens.

*If there was no moral imperative to motivate NATO, what then was the interest that drove its member countries to bomb Serbia?*

For some of the countries in the Alliance, the objective was not to lose contact with the United States. This was the case of countries like Poland, which do not have any specific interest in Kosovo, and certainly did not think that it would have to participate in a war just after it had joined NATO. Many other countries had their own particular agendas, such as Italy and France. For Great Britain, the traditional principle of its foreign policy held good, whereby it thinks it is obliged to stay one hundred percent aligned with the United States. I wouldn't say the rest is hypocrisy, because there are people who sincerely believe in what they say, but it is certainly not a serious motive for the war.

As far as the Americans are concerned, the war in Kosovo is a much more complicated question. Initially, the Americans were interested in the Balkans, because Europe had dramatically failed to stabilize the area at the beginning of the nineties. The Americans had to become involved, because at that time they understood that, as the only superpower, they could not remain on the outside. This was because at least part of the Balkans is a strategic area, and too geographically significant for the NATO structure to be ignored. Indeed, they were the first to send troops to Macedonia, back in 1992, and under Bush they explicitly declared their strategic interest to Yugoslavia, which included the fate of Kosovo. They had to do it for many reasons, not least the awareness that the United Nations would not have been able to confront and resolve the Bosnian crisis, as it is not an independent power, but based on the authority which the superpowers conferred on it. Thus, after the end of the Bosnian War, the United States found itself in a situation from which it could not disentangle itself, but in which it could not act alone without the support of the Alliance. In my opinion, the United States even saw the Bosnian crisis as an opportunity to give a new role to NATO, to give it a new purpose and meaning following the end of the Cold War, an aspiration which I haven't yet completely understood. Today, the United States considers itself to be a power that has the task of stabilizing the world, and has to resort, where necessary, to international police operations. It thus has to demonstrate that, if needed, its power can intervene anywhere on the globe, to convince potential enemies outside the NATO region.

The future of NATO is the real reason for NATO intervention. You must not forget that when Clinton listed the reasons for his decision to commence the bombing of Serbia, the first was to defend NATO's credibility, and therefore that of the United States. I don't believe that it did it very well or with great results, but it is clear that NATO felt the need to do something. In order to resolve the humanitarian crisis, there were many other kinds of action which could have been taken.

*But what then can be done to stop a dictator who can do what he wants with his people? Is military intervention to be excluded a priori?*

There are exceptions, of course. Bosnia is clearly a case in point. On the other hand, there are a few criteria which have to be followed. There have been two important examples of military intervention that have successfully halted crimes against humanity and expelled savage dictators. The first was Vietnam's invasion of Cambodia to overthrow Pol Pot's regime, and the other was Tanzania's intervention in Uganda when it was ruled by Idi Amin. I think that they were both justified. But the real reason why I don't have any reservations about these two wars is that they were successful and effective in reaching their objective, and they were over in a relatively short period of time. One of the reasons for my reservations about the intervention in Kosovo is that it was not conducted in this manner, because it was clear from the beginning that dropping a few bombs on Serbia would have worsened and aggravated the situation of the refugees. I should add that, for many years after Vietnam had brought Pol Pot's regime to an end, the United States and China continued to aid the dictator's forces, further demonstrating that the policies of states and powers are not primarily determined by ethical considerations. In the same way, I think that the humanitarian intervention in Bosnia was not really devised as such, and therefore was not effective. They announced that they would protect the Muslim enclaves, but they did not take action that could have guaranteed that objective.

I believe that, precisely because of the new fusion between domestic and international politics, intervention in the internal affairs of a state must respond to clearly defined rules and criteria. There needs to be a debate on this point: what are the new rules of the international system of powers? We need to return to a situation in which military action cannot be undertaken by anyone without there being a wide consensus and without it being based on serious justifications. The world cannot function if someone can just say, "I am strong enough to do what I want, and therefore I will do it."

*The Serbs have fought to defend the sovereignty of the nation-state. The Albanians of Kosovo rebelled because they belonged ethnically to another nation. Globalization was supposed to have heralded the end of the nation-state, and yet here it is again, shrouded even more in ethnic and religious justifications, whose roots go back into the history of the Middle Ages. What is happening?*

I think we have to distinguish between the two meanings of the term nation-state. In its traditional sense, it means a territorial state over which the people who live in it, the nation, hold a sovereign power. This is the meaning of nation-state which emerged from the French Revolution and, in part, from the American Revolution. It is a political and not an ethnic or linguistic definition of the state: it is the people who choose their government and decide to live under a certain constitution and certain laws. In comparison, the other meaning adopted for the term is much more recent, and consists of the idea that every territorial state belongs to a particular people, defined by specific ethnic, linguistic, and cultural characteristics, and this constitutes the nation. According to this idea, only one nation lives in the nation-state, and the others are minorities who live in the same place but are not part of the nation. Both types of nation-state are in crisis, but we must distinguish between them. What we find in Yugoslavia is the collapse of a state in which various nations in the ethnic sense lived together, and its transformation into several states, each of which pursues the exclusion of the other nations from its citizenship.

As far as I can see, there are actually very few signs of mass pressure from below to obtain the breakup of multinational states, at least in normal circumstances. We have seen it recently in the case of Scotland and Wales. Both these peoples, the Scots and the Welsh, are fairly clear about not being English, and they will not tolerate being defined as such, but even now that there are strong nationalist movements and even separatists in these two countries, these movements are still in the minority. To date, I cannot think of one example of secession decided by a genuinely democratic vote. I'm not saying that it's impossible, but I am saying that while there has been a lot of talk about self-determination, it has never happened in reality. When we talk about the self-determination of peoples, we should be aware of the fact that we are not talking about a strong movement from below. Naturally, once separation has occurred in reality, for whatever historical reason, it is easy to get a majority in favor, often even a large majority. Once multinational states divide and break up, then and only then are the territorial communities obliged to find new connections and to choose new loyalties.

Yugoslavia is a perfect example. It was a multinational state, and in my opinion, there was no good reason to believe that it would splinter as a result of the political pressure of its nations, no more than there was reason to believe that the Soviet Union would have exploded under the internal pressure of its nationalities. Not even in the case of the Hapsburg Empire was there a real danger of complete fragmentation, at least not until the outbreak of the war itself. The most that could be said is that there were irredentist pressures to split away to another nation in a couple of the empire's nations. For example, among the Italian and Romanian minorities, encouraged by the geographical proximity of the states to which their nationality belonged. The truth is that when empires disappear, for whatever reason, the nationalities are obliged to find alternative solutions, almost to find a justification for what has happened.

*How is history invented for nationalistic reasons, to create consensus around a regime? How is it possible for a military defeat in the fourteenth century to be turned into a founding myth of new Serbian nationalism six centuries later?*

National myths are another area where you must distinguish between what comes up from below and what is imposed from above. National myths do not arise spontaneously from people's actual experiences. They are something which people acquire from someone else: from books, from historians, from films, and now from people who make television. They are not generally part of the historical memory or a living tradition, with the exception of some special cases in which what was eventually to become a national myth was a product of religion. There is the case of the Jews, in whom the idea of expulsion from the land of Israel and the certain return to it is part of the religious practice and literature. Within certain limitations, this is also true of the Serbs, because the loss of the Serbian state in the Middles Ages became part of Orthodox religious services and nearly all the Serbian princes became symbols of the Orthodox faith. A special case. But here again, it is not a question of the people constantly remembering: they remember because someone is constantly reminding them.

The extreme example, an excellent illustration of this process, is the case of Israel. There can be no doubt that the historical myth of the expulsion from Palestine and the dream of the Jews' return was not perceived as a political program until the end of the nineteenth century. Indeed, it established itself independently of the historical fortunes of the Jewish people. For centuries, the return to Israel was not considered a practical objective, as Jews believed that they would not return to Jerusalem until the Messiah came and, of course, they believed and still believe that the Messiah has not yet come. Indeed, it was only in 1967 that, for the first time, there was a tendency within the Jewish religion to accept the State of Israel, on the grounds that the victories in the Six-Day War were so miraculous as to suggest we were actually entering the period in which the Messiah would come. It was the chance events of history which made it possible for the orthodox faith to accept something which it had completely rejected up to that time.

In fact, traditionally Zionism had always been fiercely

opposed by orthodox Jewish religion. In any case, Israel exists today, and Israel, like Zionism, has no historical foundation. Quite the contrary, it is something which goes against the entire history of the Jewish people, from the Roman Empire down to the end of the nineteenth century. The only history that Israel can use to justify itself is history that is at least two thousand years old. Everything else that has happened in the meantime is glossed over, as it does not justify the foundation of Israel and the wars which that state has fought. The fact that the Temple had been located in Jerusalem was transformed into a modern political fact, in order to argue that Jerusalem had always been the center of the Jewish religion, and therefore the capital of the Jewish people (besides, it makes little sense to talk about capitals in a period previous to the Roman Empire, but that is another question). In any case, it has been used by the Jews to justify not only the foundation of their state, but the establishment of Jerusalem as their capital.

This argument is more or less the same as the one used by the Serbs in Kosovo. In this way, a current political situation is justified by something that has nothing to do with the present, but was true six centuries or two thousand years ago. It is used to replace everything else that has happened in the intervening period. Thus a sufficiently heroic and militant history is created, which is suited to Israel in 1945 or Serbia today. The best example is what has become a kind of ritual or historical ceremony centered on the Masada rock. Masada, according to nationalistic archeologists, is the place where nine hundred Jews resisted the Romans right to the end and the moment of their collective suicide. This event has been made into a national ritual which every young Israeli takes part in, in a place where foreign tourists are taken. This process has been carried through on the whole by hiding those aspects of the story that did not suit the nationalist objective. Israel is only an example, albeit an excellent one, because Israeli archeology, which was highly politicized right from the beginning, has neglected nearly all the other aspects of local archeology to concentrate on justifying the foundations of a national and patriotic ideology.

The same thing was true in Greece. When it became independent, Athens was not in any way its capital. In reality, it had never been the capital of Greece; it had been a very important city in classical antiquity. However, it was chosen as the capital by those who, as occurred in Israel, needed to return to a glorious past with little connection to historical reality. Moreover, 50 percent of the population of Athens was then Albanian. It became what it had to become when the new Bavarian king reconstructed it in a neoclassical style, so that it could start to look like something which they pretended it had always been: the capital of a united Greece. The past, in other words, was redesigned, a little like haute couture, to put a particular political objective in smart clothing, so that the elites, the educated minorities which govern, could impose their version of history and literature on the rest of the people.

At the time of independence, the average Greek was not thinking at all about the idea of modern Greece as the heir to ancient Greece, Athens, and Pericles. Greeks did not take part in the fighting to restore classical antiquity, but more probably because they felt they were fighting in defense of the Orthodox religion against the Turks, and for the Byzantine Empire against those who had defeated it. Byzantium and the Orthodox religion were the real living traditions in Greece. Naturally, when a new state is created with a new education system, the people sooner or later learn, and to some extent, are influenced by these historical reconstructions. In the case of Greece, they even attempted to create a new literary language closer to the classical one.

There is another powerful element, which is valid everywhere, and not only in the establishment of new states. It is the need for the "permanent" and the "fundamental" which takes on a great psychological importance not only for individuals, but also for communities, particularly in the latter half of the twentieth century, an era of change and constant insecurity. Even in areas where it is not possible to live in isolation, such as the United States where wave after wave of new arrivals come to settle, we can see the emergence of a need to have priority, to be able to say, "We are here, this is our land, the others came later, and we are the ones who have always been here." It is a kind of secular version of eternity.

This reminds me of the singular example of the political movements of American Indians. Scholars of prehistory generally agree that the human race reached América by crossing the Pacific from Northeast Asia to Alaska, and then gradually colonizing the continent. This occurred relatively late on, around one hundred thousand years ago. For the activists in the Native American movement, this is for some reason a completely unacceptable theory, because it makes them too young. Thus it is possible to have publicists who say, "We don't care about what prehistory says, we have always been here, we were here before anyone else in the world." The very absurdity of this claim suggests to me that it must exercise a very powerful and sincere emotional pull. This is particularly true of people who, for other reasons, can no longer be certain either of being unique or of always remaining where they are, because they are subject to a continuous intermingling and movement around the globe.

For some reason, it is considered an advantage from the point of view of social psychology to be able to boast a long history. This is why nationalism, in spite of being a young phenomenon, invariably claims to be very ancient. This is because a venerable old age satisfies the need for permanence and rights of precedence over others. It is therefore an extremely complex phenomenon, which we can only explain through approximations, and there are no single convincing interpretations.

# 2) The Decline
# of the Western Empire

*The nationalistic outbursts, which you have just analyzed, are however accompanied by the disintegration of states in many parts of the world, the collapse of institutions and legal systems and their replacement by the rule of violent bands and ethnic groups. At the other extreme, they can be simply replaced, as in the case of tax havens, by management boards for global capitalism. What is the future of the state as an institution in the next century?*

I think we are faced with the reversal of a centuries-long process, the long historical wave which moved toward the construction and gradual strengthening of territorial states or nation-states in the political sense of the term. It is a trend that has dominated the developed world at least since the sixteenth century up to, I would say, around the 1960s. The interesting thing is that this process has developed completely without reference to the ideological nature of states, particularly since the eighteenth century. It applied to all regimes, irrespective of whether they were liberal, conservative, fascist, or anything else. The state became increasingly capable of defining the area and the population that it governed, it provided itself with an ever-growing mass of information relating to its sovereignty, and it became more effective in its administrative duties. In other words, it acquired knowledge and power, enlarged its ambitions, and widened its range of responsibilities and areas of intervention. When this process reached its zenith in the middle of the Short Century, there was very little that the state did not control.

You'll remember the English sociologist Thomas Marshall's theory of citizenship: first comes civil and legal citizenship and the citizenship of rights, then political citizenship, which involves participation, and finally social citizenship. For the state, this means that it took over a monopoly of the law and transformed it into state law. Then politics became national politics and all other forms of politics were subordinated to it or came to depend on it. Finally, the state widened its field of activity, starting with control over its own army, at least since the seventeenth century, and ending up with the management of industries, and indeed the planning of entire economies, so that almost nothing remained outside its control. I am not referring here to totalitarianism. The United Kingdom, the most liberal state in the early eighteenth century, was already enormously powerful, not only in knowing what was happening within its territory, but also in administering it.

Up until the nineteenth century, no state was capable of carrying out an accurate census. Before that, it was virtually impossible to have a system that could effectively monitor the rural population. It had even been difficult to know the precise positions of the territorial borders of national sovereignty. In spite of the Pyrenees constituting a very clear dividing line, the frontier between Spain and France was not determined in detail until the Treaty of 1868. This tendency of territorial states to increase their precision, knowledge, technical capacity, power, and ambition continued almost uninterrupted, even through the period of laissez-faire economics, right up to the end of the 1960s.

Take two examples: one is the extraordinary success achieved in the nineteenth century by all the leading states in the world in the disarmament of their people. In other words, they granted a monopoly over the means of coercion to their own agencies. Before then, it was easier to disarm peasants than nobles. Machiavelli discussed this problem at length. In the nineteenth century, the ability of the majority of states to prevent the inhabitants from going around armed is truly remarkable. One of the few exceptions was the United States, which chose not to do so, although it could have. In Canada, for example, it was carried out. The other example is public order, which is part of the same phenomenon. The degree of public order in the developed countries of Europe was a quite extraordinary historical event.

There is another element, which occurred not so much with the arrival of democracy as with the involvement of ordinary people in the political process. This element was the voluntary loyalty and subordination of citizens to their own governments. This was loyalty not to patricians, but to the state and the nation. Wars based on conscription would not have been possible without this. You will perhaps recall what Thomas Hobbes wrote: "The only thing which no state, not even the Leviathan, can do is to force people to kill and be willing to be killed." Yet modern states managed to do precisely this, and to do it repeatedly. Although they often did this through conscription, they also managed it by appealing to each citizen and convincing them that, if they identified with the collectivity, they had to be ready for that supreme act of surrendering their liberty and life. Voluntary obedience to the state has been an essential element in the capacity to mobilize populations, and also of democratization. This process developed over centuries, and reached its highest point in the 1960s, when all countries in the world, including the most capitalist ones, were structured as states with enormous powers. This was even truer of the United States than elsewhere.

This tendency appears to have come to a halt. I don't know whether it has been reversed, but it certainly has lost its momentum since the 1960s. Let's be clear about this, it is not so much that the power of the state is being restricted, at least in theory. Indeed, its ability to find out what is happening within its territory, and to control it, is greater than ever before. The state is now capable of listening to virtually every conversation, even one at the top of a mountain. We are witnessing an enormous growth in the use of video cameras operating on a twenty-four-hour basis, which watch over every public space. The degree of surveillance that is now possible is greater and more penetrating than ever before in history. I wouldn't say, therefore, that the state has lost power.

Yet it has, for example, lost to some extent its monopoly over the means of coercion. This is partly because of the considerable availability of certain kinds of weapons today, but it is also because the reluctance of citizens to use them has diminished, which I believe to be particularly significant. In other words, the change is that citizens are less willing to obey the laws of the state than in the past. I think that one of the first examples of this phenomenon was '68. If you compare the behavior of the New Left students and radicals in the American courts with the previous attitude of the communist defendants, you'll notice that, although the latter refused to provide information against themselves and appealed to the Fifth Amendment, they behaved more or less in accordance with the rules, which ultimately they accepted. The New Left, on the other hand, did not conform to the rules, rejected the whole procedure, and acted as though they no longer recognized the fundamental principles that uphold the conduct of public affairs, which had all previously been considered the duty of every citizen.

Another example is public order. In the seventies, British police superintendents informed the government that it would no longer be possible to guarantee the level of internal peace and public order that had been ensured until then. The demonstrations against the Vietnam War were another example: they were more like revolts than peaceful demonstrations. The strength of the modern state reached its peak when social protest was in some way institutionalized as part of the normal political process, almost as though it were a ritual. This also came to an end in 1970s Europe.

Clear evidence of this phenomenon has been the inability over long periods of time to eliminate armed forces organized within the state's own national territory, even where strong government exists. For example, the IRA represented for thirty years the coexistence in Northern Ireland of a normal state administration and elements of the territory's government that were outside its control. This was in spite of the fact that, compared with the state, the IRA had infinitely less men and arms at its disposal. This may be a temporary phenomenon, but what is certain is that it has been reinforced since the seventies by governments imbued with a theological belief in the supremacy of free markets, which was directed explicitly against the state in order to weaken it and deliberately reverse the historical trend of an increasingly powerful role for states in the economy and its other responsibilities in general.

This does not mean that states disintegrated. In spite of

having had to live with a situation of almost civil war between factions for thirty years, Great Britain has not disintegrated, although it has possibly been weakened. However,
I do maintain that this marked a change in the relationship
between state and non-state activities within its territory.

The other part of the problem is to be found in those regions of the world where all forms of state are tending to
disappear. We now have (and I think this is something quite
new) large areas of Africa and considerable parts of Western
and Central Asia where it is practically impossible to speak
of a functional state. Perhaps the same is also true of the
Balkans. It is not clear to what extent we can talk today of a
functional state in Albania. The contrast is surprising, because, whether we like it or not, there was a state in Albania
until the demise of communism, just as there was, but
clearly no longer is, in the North Caucasus. I think that both
this reversal in the process of strengthening nation-states
over several centuries and the disintegration and effective
disappearance of some states are linked to the sovereign
state's loss of its virtual monopoly over coercive force. In
some cases, such as Afghanistan, there is no longer any state.
Its place has been taken by feuds between factions which are
armed to various degrees and linked to a greater or lesser
extent to aristocrats and landowners. Such factions fight it
out in order to achieve a kind of balance, as occurred with
fifteenth-century feudalism. Elsewhere, in Africa, for instance, even this is not the case.

I believe that the disintegration of states in these regions
of the world is mainly the result of the collapse of the colonial empires, of the end of the era in which the great European powers controlled large portions of the world, where
they had found non-state-governed societies, and had imposed a degree of external and internal order. This also ap-

plies to the territories conquered by Russia after 1800, such as the Caucasus. It is now clear that only in a few cases was this process anything more than an imposition from outside. In Albania, for example, where there was no state before 1913 because there was no Albania, there can be no doubt that there was a functional state under the communist regime, even if it was perhaps the product of some compromise with non-state powers. But as soon as that regime disappeared de facto, Albania was plunged back into a system of clan warfare, as occurred in Chechnya.

What has occurred in these parts of the world seems to me to be similar in some ways to what occurred in Western Europe following the fall of the Roman Empire. There was no longer any central authority. In some cases, there were local authorities which still managed to function, and in other cases there was conquest by groups from outside which came in to establish themselves. However, in reality vast regions of Europe lacked normal and permanent state structures for a long period of time. I believe that this is occurring again in parts of the world. This creates serious problems in relations with the other parts of the globe where this is not occurring: Europe, America, and Eastern Asia. It raises the question of interaction between the world where the state exists and the world where it does not.

It is difficult to say whether the world will become even more difficult to manage for this reason or also because of the problem I mentioned earlier; namely, the obedience of people to their governments. For most of history, there was a general assumption that citizens would obey effective government, whatever that government was, and whether they approve of it or not. It is true that in some cases it was accepted because it was strong, but in other cases it was accepted on the basis of the idea expressed by Hobbes, according to which any effective government is better than no government at all. For example, when the British conquered India, they managed to rule that country for a very long period with little more than a few ten thousands of men, including soldiers. Given that they were governing a country of hundreds of millions of people, this would have been impossible if the majority of the population had not decided to accept the regime. Indians had accepted others in the past, who had been equally foreign, and they accepted it this time too. This is the reason for the extraordinary success of the majority of the European powers in ruling vast colonial empires. Ultimately, very few peoples resisted, and certainly not those who were already accustomed to living under a government of one kind or another. Only the peoples who lived in stateless societies refused to submit: as in the case of Afghanistan, the tribal societies of the Wild West, the Kurds, or the Berbers of Morocco. Basically, the peoples who resisted were peoples who would have resisted any form of government, whether their own or foreign. What I mean is that the majority of peoples in the world accepted the idea of being governed.

The new situation, at the close of the Short Century and following the mobilization of people from below (because this has been the century of the common people, in which people have taken on an essential role in the administration of the res publica, or public thing), is that you can no longer take for granted this readiness to accept higher authority. In a way, the Resistance during the Second World War in Europe was a foretaste of this phenomenon. The traditional reaction to conquest from outside was that of Pétain and Vichy France: we have lost, they have won, and we must accept the situation. A rational reaction. However, the

Resistance movement completely refused to conform to this. This was the beginning of the change.

This is the reason why it seems to me that the obvious solution implemented in the nineteenth century in those areas of the world where states were disintegrating, which consisted of transforming them into colonies, will no longer work. It is too costly and the results are uncertain. Look at the example I gave in my *Age of Extremes:* Somalia. The British and Italians always had problems in that country, but at no time did they have serious difficulty in governing it as a colony. Nobody even suggested that they should withdraw. In the nineties, the United States intervened for humanitarian reasons, and before they had time to take their bearings, they had already been thrown out. People in many countries of the world are no longer willing to accept the principle that it is not worthwhile fighting against armies of occupation.

This is also true in the Balkans. In the past, the argument was that a small country, when faced with the clear and overwhelming superiority of its adversary, sooner or later had to say, "All right, there's not a lot that can be done to stop them." This was also partly rational, but it so happens that this no longer occurs so easily. It will therefore become increasingly difficult to know what to do in these areas, because effective intervention would require the permanent mobilization of forces which very few countries would be ready to maintain, or would only do so if their survival was at risk. For instance, Great Britain would never mobilize the same resources for an action in Kosovo that it has used in Northern Ireland, because it is not as important. If you compare the cost of governing Bosnia after its war, with the cost of ruling a colony, you will realize that the difference is out of all proportion. I believe there were 64,000 foreign soldiers in tiny Bosnia, which was more or less the number required by the British to govern and maintain order in the Indian Sub-Continent.

*The unresolved problem of Central and Eastern Europe is at the center of the European crisis, which promptly reexploded once the fragile veil of the Soviet Empire was torn away by the fall of the Berlin Wall. You have said that when you were born there only existed six of the twenty-three states that currently appear on the map between Trieste and the Urals, and someone of your age who was born in the city currently called Lviv [Lemberg, Lwow, L'vov, L'viv] would have lived under four states, without counting the occupying regimes during the war. Is then uncertainty the fate of these peoples and this part of Europe? It appears that the attempt at multinational coexistence by Stalin's Soviet Union and Tito's Yugoslavia hasn't left a single trace in these peoples' consciousness.*

We don't yet know what will be the long-term effect of these regimes on the people which they governed, although it is clear that there will be long-term effects. For instance, we are not seeing any movement among Russian peasants for a return to private enterprise in agriculture, even though private agriculture was a paradise for the Russian peasantry before collectivization in the twenties. There are other effects that have been protracted over generations. I recently read an article on Russian Jews in Israel which claimed that, unlike the other Jews, they arrived in Israel without any sense of inferiority, unaffected by the Holocaust syndrome. Their general attitude was expressed in these terms: "We fought Hitler and we defeated him." This was in spite of the anti-Semitism they suffered in Russia. Moreover, these Jews were much more secular than others. There were permanent and lasting effects on the peoples who lived under these regimes for many decades. However, we do not have adequate research to establish what the effects are and how far-reaching they will be.

Of course, the reappearance of dramatic nationalist hostilities in these countries is in some ways inexplicable, particularly because they seemed to have almost disappeared due to the high number of mixed marriages, especially in the cities. It is probable that this phenomenon was more common among the educated classes than in the poorer parts of those societies, but its spread and magnitude were such that you would not have expected this new separation and segregation of ethnic groups.

In *The Age of Extremes*, I spoke about one factor which might help us to understand: the communist regimes were in a way deliberately elitist regimes, if for no other reason than that they insisted on the Party's leading role. Their purpose was not to convert the people; they were not so much faiths as official churches. For this reason, the majority of the peoples subjected to these regimes were fundamentally depoliticized. Communism did not enter into their lives in the sense that Catholicism, for example, entered into the consciousness of Latin American peoples following colonization. Communism was something of which good and bad results were expected, but which, generally, was not internalized by these peoples. There was one real exception, and that was Greater Russia in the Second World War. There can be little doubt that Stalin managed to transform himself into a true national leader because he directed a war that the people genuinely perceived as national. It was a war in which virtually every Russian was involved. This is why you still have to devote a great deal of attention to the experience of the war when asking questions about Communism's legacy in Russia.

In any case, when these states collapsed, exactly as happened when the other empires fragmented after the Great War, everyone had to find different connections and solidarities. Even those who did not want to had to do so. Where forms of nationalism had previously existed, which perhaps weren't necessarily anti-Soviet, they were obliged by history to fulfill a new, more powerful, and more prominent role. Paradoxically, the communists had accepted the nationalist criterion of territories "belonging to" an ethnically and linguistically defined nation. Hence in multinational territories the empire consisted officially of federations of such "nations." When it broke down, it therefore cracked along these already constituted fault lines. Perhaps the resurgence of nationalism was something already written into the genetic code of those societies. It is possible that the national divisions continued to operate at a much deeper level than we supposed. Yet I cannot believe that the peaceful coexistence of the Yugoslavian peoples for fifty years was due entirely and exclusively to the authority of the Yugoslavian Communist Party.

*Should we be worried about a world that is no longer governed by an international system of states, as we have known since the eighteenth century?*

Ideally speaking, we could prefer a different system. It is also true that progressives are not agreed on a single way of organizing states and political units. There could be others, apart from those we are already familiar with. But yes, we should also be worried, because globalization is a process that cannot easily be applied to politics. We can have a globalized economy, we can aspire to a globalized culture, we certainly have a globalized technology and a single global science, but politically speaking, we have a world that remains in reality pluralist and divided into territorial states. It is true that not all these states are the same. There are around two hundred on the face of this earth, of which a certain number are tax havens and in reality have no reason for existing other than their usefulness to the global economy. However, three-quarters of the world's population live in around twenty-five states with more than fifty million inhabitants each.

While in theory it is possible to have an assortment of global institutions, I do not believe it is possible for politics to operate in such a vacuum. The reality is that there are no global political institutions. The nearest thing to such an institution, the United Nations, derives its power from existing states. In the current situation, there is therefore a coexistence of two different systems: one for the economy, and one for politics. It is in this context that you have to ask yourself what will be the effect of weakening the nation-state. Is it a good or a bad thing? We will see. But it is certain that nation-states cannot be ignored, and you cannot examine the world as though they did not exist or were not important, because in politics nothing exists besides them. The possibility of a single global authority carrying out an effective political and military role is currently nonexistent.

*Do you regret the passing of a bipartisan structure of two superpowers, who supervised their own areas of influence and acted as policemen? What did you think when the USSR dissolved, given that it was a player on the international scene that you looked on sympathetically as an element of emancipation and stability?*

The problem of the Cold War was that the world lived constantly under the shadow of a lethal catastrophe, nuclear world war. While the Cold War lasted, and that was a long period, the possibilities of such a catastrophe were very high for one reason or another, not least as an accident. You know Murphy's Law, which says that if something could go wrong, it almost certainly will sooner or later. The fact that it threatened nuclear war was the main reason for being against the Cold War. It did not happen, although there were some moments in which it could have (the Cuban missile crisis, and, in my opinion, the early eighties). However, we avoided it. We must admit that the Cold War stabilized the world, or at least stabilized large parts of the world, for better or worse according to your point of view. The majority of European countries think it was a good thing. I don't know if the same can be said of parts of Asia; for example, I don't know whether it was a good thing that Indonesia was stabilized for thirty years under Suharto. There's no denying it stabilized the world. It did not make war impossible, but, exactly as occurred in the nineteenth century, it made some kinds of war at least manageable. As this state of affairs no longer exists, we have to ask ourselves what could replace it.

For the moment, it has been replaced by complete uncertainty, because not only has the Soviet Union been totally destroyed, but also the entire system of international relations to which the world, or at least Europe, has been accustomed since the eighteenth century at the latest. In practice, this system was founded on the existence of certain players, countries that fulfilled a primary role. Everyone knew who they were and generally which side they were on. This included Russia, which from the early eighteenth century was always of more or less the same size territorially. Moreover, people knew the rules of the game, which had existed since the end of the Thirty Years' War and the Treaty of Westphalia in 1648, 350 years ago. The autonomy and sovereignty of individual states was recognized, and people knew when it was possible to interfere in their affairs, and what you could and couldn't do in international politics. Both these elements have now disappeared.

We have already spoken of the erosion of rules; for example, the difference between war and peace, the principle of noninterference, the prohibition on crossing borders except in times of war (because the basic rule was not that you could not simply wage war, but that you had to declare it). But another aspect of the problem is the disappearance of the old powers, which has left an enormous vacuum. Russia is still continuing to disintegrate as a state. This is something that had not occurred since the middle of the seventeenth century. Since the early eighteenth century, between Poland and the Pacific Ocean there was a single entity, which might have had many problems and considerable uncertainties in the Central Asian regions, but it was a single identifiable unit. Today, this no longer exists. Even conceptually, we have lost this idea. We can no long say that, whatever else occurs in the future, Russia will be one of the principal players on the international stage. Even after the tragic defeats of 1918 and 1945, we were able to say, "All right, now it's on its knees, but it's clear that sooner or later Germany will again be a major player," but you could not say the same of Russia today. Its tragedy is so great that even its future existence is in question. The true magnitude of this catastrophe has been seriously underestimated.

There have been three breaks in the history of the European continent during this century: after the First World War, during and after the Second, and after the collapse of the Soviet Union. Well, I think that the latter is definitely the one that will have the greatest long-term effects. We do not yet know what these will be. For instance, politically the future of the states that succeeded the Soviet Union is still uncertain. We are not ten years from the collapse of the USSR, and they are still disintegrating. They are divided into mutually hostile groups, as in Central Asia, and their structure is very vague. The political future of Tajikistan is not at all clear, like its neighbor Afghanistan, which has been engaged in a civil war for many years. The Russian Federation itself continues to disintegrate into autonomous and practically independent areas. Thus the political destiny of the part of the world that extends from its border with Romania to its one with China is dramatically uncertain. This did not occur after the two world wars. The question for 2000 is what could be the effective replacement for the old system of powers that ruled the world.

*America perhaps. The century that is ending has been called the American century. Now the United States appears to be devising the task of managing the world order on a planetary scale, using NATO as the military arm of this ambition. In the case of Kosovo, they claimed to act outside pure strategic interests and on the basis of humanitarian rhetoric. Are we therefore heading toward another American century, which this time will be "ethical" as well?*

It is possible, but I doubt it. It seems to me that the American century is above all based on the enormous predominance, dynamism, and size of the economy of the United States. It is of a magnitude that cannot be compared with the other capitalist nations. We should remember that in the twenties it already accounted for 40 percent of the world's total industrial capacity. It lost part of this advantage during the Great Depression and recovered after the Second World War to the point where for a period it represented half of the economic power of all the other countries put together. I believe that this is going to end. Relatively speaking, America will be demographically smaller, and it already represents a smaller portion of the world's productive capacity. Of course, it does have control of a large part of the global economy, both politically and through the hegemony of the American model of business and entrepreneurial organization. In spite of this, I very much doubt that America can continue to be the industrial engine of the world, at least in the manner in which it has been for the large part of the twentieth century, just as Great Britain, at a given point in its history, ceased to be the major capitalist power, because it was not big enough to remain so. With the generalized industrialization of vast areas of the world, the relative force of America as a productive system will decline.

The second reason for the American century has been its cultural hegemony, especially in terms of popular culture. This has a better chance of perpetuating itself, because it has been reinforced by the increasing role of the English language and the spread of computer technology, which has been standardized using English, and is overwhelmingly concentrated in America. Thus it will certainly last. However, cultural hegemony has its limits. Think of Italy's domination of music in the seventeenth and eighteenth centuries. It had no political, military, or economic support, yet it was total. In the end, however, it disappeared. We could look, for instance, at British cultural hegemony in the nineteenth century. Practically every sport that is played in the world today was originally invented and played in Great Britain. Male fashion was created in England. Today, people still play football everywhere in the world, and men dress in the English manner, yet Great Britain is no longer the leader in either football or fashion. So we can perceive this phenomenon as an historical event and not a current one.

However, there is a difference: unlike Great Britain in the nineteenth century, America is a revolutionary power, based on a revolutionary ideology. Like revolutionary France and Soviet Russia, America is not just a state, it is also a state dedicated to the transformation of the world in a certain manner. In this sense, American cultural hegemony has a political dimension which British hegemony never had. The British, even at the zenith of their power, never attempted to convert the world. On the other hand, this ambition, this tendency to be a global model, is inherent in the American system. In short, the fact that America will obviously stay the major power does not mean by itself that the next century will be an American one. But it will not be anybody else's century, because the one thing that seems increasingly clear is that the world has become too large and complicated to be dominated by a single state.

You will remember the argument that Bobbio used in the debate over the war in Kosovo, when he claimed that there has always been a hegemonic power, which at the moment is America, and that this is a good thing because America is now on the right side. I don't believe that there has always been a hegemonic power. First of all, global hegemony was simply out of the question until the eighteenth century. Even after that, no country exercised such a claim before the Americans did it in the latter part of the twentieth century.

British hegemony, which was very strong economically, culturally, and in some ways, militarily (Great Britain had a fleet that was larger than all the other fleets in the world put together), was never such that it drove Great Britain to attempt the organization of the world. They did what they could to regulate it according to their own interests, but not to dominate it, because the British knew they were not strong enough to do so, or even to maintain their most precious asset: the fleet. They were aware that eventually there would be other countries rich and strong enough to provide themselves with an equivalent military control of the seas. Thus America is the only country in history that has been in a position to claim world hegemony.

Even regional hegemonies are very rare. With the exception of China in the Far East, they have not, in most cases, been long-lasting. The idea of a European hegemony has always been a short-lived dream, and rarely lasted more than a few years. There was no Spanish hegemony in the sixteenth century, because France was always a potential contender, and there was no French hegemony in the seventeenth century, although Louis XIV came close. Under Napoleon and Hitler, a power at war dominated the Continent, but neither lasted for more than a few years. I believe, as a historian, that the idea of a single power, however great and powerful, being able to control world politics is a mistake. America attempted to do this, and is still trying. This is primarily because of its revolutionary aspirations to transform the world, which were inscribed in its origins, but also because of the historical accident of finding itself in a world in which no other country or alliance is capable of fighting a war against it. This is a gamble, and, for my part, it is a dangerous gamble. In other words, there is a risk behind the

American aspiration to become the world policeman, or to establish a new world order.

*Could the ethic of libertarian individualism, which motivates the markets, be applied to foreign policy? It is founded on the priority of individuals in relation to the community of which they are part. It is therefore intrinsically liberal. Could it represent a serious antidote to all communitarian ideologies, including their nationalistic and ethnic deviations?*

I believe that libertarian individualism is not a suitable basis for power politics, because it is fundamentally opposed to collective politics. People can be mobilized on the basis of nationalism, patriotism, or other collective terrains. But if you argue that the interests of individuals are supreme, it is then difficult to persuade them to subordinate those interests even partially to the interests of others. The logic of libertarian individualism is perfectly compatible with the free market, but I do not think it is with the requirements of international politics. I do not believe that American politics or the politics of any other country were really determined or dominated by this ideal.

The only way in which this appeal could work was the one used by America during the Cold War, when the government gave its people the following message: our credo of individualism and liberalism is threatened by an external force and we must therefore act in self-defense. This is a strategy for legitimizing foreign policy, but is not in itself a foreign policy. It is possible, given that it was a successful policy, that the United States will attempt to use it again. Indeed, following the Cold War, which eliminated the greatest enemy of American values, there are some people in America who identify other cultural forces, such as fundamentalism and Orientalism, as new external threats against which they should mobilize. But it does not seem a very convincing argument, because the strength of the Cold War and its justification was the fact that the potential aggressor to American ideals and interests was a real and formidable superpower.

Perhaps, when and if China should really become a dangerous superpower, this appeal might work again. But I have to say that I cannot see the universal fascination for this argument. It is strictly limited to the rich countries. Clearly, it is an argument that would not have the same effect in most of the Third World. This is why I don't believe that libertarian individualism is a political antidote. Look at the case of Kosovo. On the basis of this doctrine, you cannot ask anyone to sacrifice his life. The prevailing theory in the United States that you can do anything except ask your soldiers to get themselves killed is entirely compatible with the conviction that individual rights are supreme. However, the reality is that this is no way to wage war. You can bomb in this manner, but you cannot fight. On occasions, bombing might not be sufficient.

*But isn't it safer for the world to have a single superpower?*

The problem is understanding what limitations there are on a single superpower. What it can do and what it cannot do. We have already said that it cannot determine what happens in the world, but it can take certain measures to moderate conflicts and stabilize the international situation. Here it would be useful to compare British hegemony in the nineteenth century with the American one in the twentieth century. As an aside, the British hegemony in the nineteenth century was the model that the Americans tried to follow in the twentieth century. The very expression "Pax Americana" is an echo of "Pax Britannica," just as this had been an echo of "Pax Romana."

I think that the British knew that there were limits on what a medium-sized country could do. For instance, the British knew that there were regions of the world where it was worse to intervene with military force. They became convinced of this fairly early, in the nineteenth century. For example, they ruled out all military interventions in South America, even though they had been, however, very involved in the conflicts against Spain. It was clear to the British that they should not intervene in the Americas against the USA. They accepted the Monroe Doctrine, but not because they had to, given that for most of the nineteenth century they were certainly not weaker than the USA. There was, for example, a dispute over British Guiana [Guyana] that the Americans resolved in a manner which was unsatisfactory for Great Britain. The British accepted, because ultimately they understood that there are limits on what can be achieved in the world. Equally, they never attempted to establish a form of supremacy within Europe. They were solely interested in stopping any other power from doing so: the balance of power.

The British always concentrated on controlling the seas and occupying pieces of the world that were essential to this end, which they fully succeeded in doing. The empire was founded on small islands annexed for strategic purposes by Britain: Gibraltar, Malta, the Falklands, and many others which even now are under its direct control. On the other hand, the American Empire based its hegemony on satellite states, which the British never attempted to do, unless it was a necessary alternative to colonization. They did it in India, West Africa, and to some extent the Middle East, but only when colonization was impossible. From 1800, the United States never thought in terms of colonization outside North America. The occupation of Puerto Rico and the Philippines was a historical accident and perhaps a concession to the colonial fashion of the time. The idea of the Americans was rather to have a wide number of states, especially in Latin America, that were obliged to do what they wanted them to.

I think therefore that the British knew their own limitations, and the Americans were affected by a kind of megalomania, because they thought they could do anything they wanted in the Western Hemisphere, partly because for much of the nineteenth century there were no global politics, but hemispheric politics at the very most. The Americans even expressed this view. In 1895, the American secretary of state declared after the solution of the frontier dispute between Venezuela and British Guiana that: "Today the United States is practically sovereign on this continent and its fiat is law upon the subjects to which it confines its interposition. Why? . . . It is because, in addition to all other grounds, its infinite resources combined with its isolated position render it master of the situation and practically invulnerable as against any and all other powers." No British foreign minister, not even Palmerston, would have ever said such a thing in any part of the world: we are a universal power, no one can interfere, and if we decide to do something, we can do it.

I believe the danger represented by the Americans is that they have extended this view to the whole world. It is a grave danger, because it is now clear that the United States

act without allies, if only because their military bases
many cases in other countries. Theoretically, if Italy
decided not to provide its military airports for the war in
Yugoslavia, this would have been extremely embarrassing
for American power. I believe that they have often won-
dered, in Iraq or the Balkans, for example, what they could
do without their bases in allied countries. They would only
be able to take action with aircraft carriers or nonstop flights
from the United States. The U.S. must have allies, someone
ready to help them.

In the second place, their most powerful arms, which are
the high-tech ones, are not always sufficient to win wars.
Consequently, it appears to me that American policy will
have to adapt to this reality in the next century, along the
lines of British policy in the past. It will have to adapt to the
limits on the achievable. It will remain a superpower for a
very, very long time. I cannot even see an end to that period,
as far as military technology is concerned. But even this will
not be enough. It would be enough if the threat of a massive
superiority were sufficient to make its adversaries say,
"There is nothing that can be done, we must give up." This
was the dilemma of Iraq and Kosovo. The sooner the United
States recognize this, the sooner they will devise a policy for
a superpower: the show of force is not enough to govern the
world.

This is now true of both superpowers or regional powers,
because the peoples of the weaker countries are no longer
willing to submit to it. I recently had the opportunity to discuss the problems of Central Africa with some British dip-
lomats who were professionally involved in the situation.
The entire African policy has been destroyed by the refusal
of the countries in this region to play the game according to
the rules. There was a time when if something went wrong

in an independent African state, the French would send in a battalion of parachutists, they made them parade through the main city, they showed their military power, the bad guys ran away, and the old president was restored or the new president was installed. Order was completely reestablished. This can no longer be done. What happened in Rwanda was that the French were there, ready to act and wishing to stop the massacre of the Tutsi. They were in reality allies of the Hutu, but they didn't want a bloodbath. They did their best to show that they did not want it, but it was of no use. The Hutu simply told themselves that the French could do nothing, and continued to murder their neighbors practically under the eyes of the French.

In the end, a whole vast area of Central Africa was completely transformed, but not by the actions of some power or international organization. Everyone got involved: Paris, Washington, and the United Nations. Everyone tried to mediate, and at one stage, there were, I am told, as many as thirteen different mediators in Rwanda. However, it all proved to be inadequate. Zaire, Rwanda, Burundi, Uganda: as many as seven African states became involved in the war. Any external intervention would have been—I won't say costly—but it would not have obtained results proportional to the effort put in. This situation would also have been valid for the United States, even though they are so rich that they can afford the commitment of vast resources. There are many things in the world that simply cannot be done.

*What new superpower could appear in the new century?*

It is very probable that China will become a great power, even in the military sense, and it is certainly the only single

55

state that could aspire to compete with the United States in the future. However, I believe that, at the moment, it is extremely improbable to see it competing with America in military terms in the foreseeable future. The United States's advantage is too great. I don't think that this excludes the possibility of a nuclear confrontation, because this has never been based on equality, but simply on the fact that one of the sides has enough deterrent to threaten intolerable damage on the other. In any event, we have to consider it an established fact that for a very long time the United States will remain the greatest military power. Besides, any conflict between the United States and China in the twenty-first century might perhaps take on forms different from those of the past. This is mainly because China is essentially a land power. This is speculation, so it is too perilous for a historian to say much.

As far as India is concerned, I think that the nuclear arms are directed against Pakistan. Their interest is regional, and India is a regional power. It is unlikely that it will become anything more than that in the next fifty years. In some ways, India has an extremely promising future principally because it has an asset that China does not have: a degree of true originality in the fields of technology and intellectual research, which for historical reasons, is not easy to find in the Far East in the Confucian area. For example, the Indians have had a very important philosophical and mathematical tradition. On the other hand, the degree to which China and Japan have a philosophical tradition, at least in the European sense, is arguable. In a modern society based on technology, intellectual originality has enormous potential. India's great difficulty is that the state is considerably weak in its structure, administrative ability, and political system.

But, economically and culturally, I think that India has a brilliant future, more than other countries in the Far East.

*The pope has explicitly expressed his disagreement with the domination of the American superpower. After having aimed his attacks against communism, he now appears to have chosen capitalism in its extreme American form as his enemy. How do you judge John Paul II as a historical figure? Is he the last revolutionary on the face of the earth? Or are we faced with a modern version of the conflict between the papacy and the empire?*

I do not think that we are faced with a conflict between the papacy and the empire. I believe that we have to distinguish between the pope's politics and theology. John Paul II is a Catholic traditionalist. This papacy marks a return to a more traditional view of the Church than that of the relatively liberal Catholicism of the sixties and seventies. How far this is possible, I don't know. If I were pope, I would probably do the same thing, because if religion has a future, then it is precisely in not changing with the changing times, and in keeping aloof from fashions. But I am not religious, and therefore the subject does not directly concern me.

However, I think that this restoration project will encounter very serious and possibly insurmountable difficulties because, just as the state can no longer totally control its citizenry, so the Catholic Church can no longer command the loyalty of its believers. The problem with an authoritarian religion like Catholicism is that it is based on a voluntary acceptance of its theology. I believe that since the women of Catholic Europe have ceased to accept automatically the moral teachings or dictates of the Church, the possibilities of governing the whole of Christianity have been drastically diminished, and will have to be transferred from the developed countries to the Third World. But not all the Third World would do, as the weakness of the Church in Latin America also emerged in the twentieth century. The Catholic Church in Europe has not been immune to the secularization and decline of traditional mass religion. Since the mid-sixties, its hold over its believers has been seriously weakened.

There is however something important about this pope, something that recalls the great papacies of the late nineteenth century, and the power of *"Rerum Novarum."* John Paul II is the last great ideologue to criticize capitalism for what it is. This is perhaps a historical accident, because I believe that the secular left will return to its critical view of capitalism. In the last ten years, it has been too frightened to say that capitalism is a moral evil. I think it will start saying it again. Yet, at the moment, the pope is the only figure of world importance who systematically rejects capitalism. This is certainly eccentric in relation to Western conformist thought and the dominant political and intellectual consensus. It is a very interesting phenomenon.

*Often, as in the war in Kosovo, we witness a strange alliance under the standard of the papacy between the extreme Left and the extreme Right, who are united by their anti-Americanism. Doesn't this disturb you?*

No, at least not in principle. You can find many unusual alliances throughout history. The most extraordinary of all in the twentieth century was the alliance between the United States and the Soviet Union against Nazi Germany. At that time, the Catholic Church was more on the other side. The fact that strange alliances can be formed does not mean that they have to be permanent. It is more interesting to note in the case of Kosovo that the division did not occur along the traditional lines of Left and Right, and cut across national and ideological boundaries. The Left was certainly divided. Different groups on the Left took up strong positions for and against the war. But the same thing happened on the Right, although I think that they criticized the war mainly from the point of view of military professionalism, because it was badly executed.

In the pope's case, his condemnation of the war was certainly not for pacifist reasons. In general, I do not believe that the majority of the people who criticized the war did so out of pacifism. They opposed this particular war as a solution for this particular problem. However, it is true that anti-Americanism and suspicion over the hegemonic ambitions of a single state were the factor that united a wide variety of political positions. It's not that I'm happy about it; I am simply emphasizing that this is how things are, and the war in Kosovo has strengthened this sentiment.

# 3) The Global Village

*The distinctive feature of the last decade of the twentieth century has been the globalization of the economy. Do you believe that the world is already a global entity, a single economic unit?*

No. We are certainly a single global economy compared with thirty years ago, but we can say with equal certainty that we will be even more globalized in 2050, and very much more in 2100. Globalization is not the product of a single action, like switching on a light or starting a car engine. It is a historical process that has undoubtedly speeded up enormously in the last ten years, but it is a permanent, constant transformation. It is not at all clear, therefore, at what stage we can say it has reached its final destination and can be considered complete. This is principally because it essentially involves expanding across a globe that is by its very nature varied geographically, climatically, and historically. This reality imposes certain limitations on the unification of the entire planet. However, we are all agreed that globalization, and especially the globalized economy, has made such spectacular progress that today you couldn't talk of an international division of labor as we did before the seventies.

*Yet it seems that globalization, in spite of its success, is still restricted by the existence of states and their power. How else could we interpret the unsuccessful attempt made through the Multilateral Agreement on Investment to give transnational corporations the unilateral right to sue states for any policy that damaged their profits? Why does this antagonism remain?*

I think this happens because globalization isn't a universal process that operates in all fields of human activity in the same way. While you could say there is a natural historical trend toward globalization for technology, communications, and the economy, this is certainly not true of politics. We are comparing different aspects of the world, which do not develop in the same manner.

*What then do you mean exactly by globalization? The general reply is to point to two factors: the reduction or total elimination of trade barriers between states, and the liberalization of capital markets, which allows them to go anywhere they can find higher returns. However, the world has already known these phenomena: if I am not mistaken, capitalism before the Great War had both these characteristics. What then is really new about it?*

First, I don't think that you can identify globalization solely with the creation of a global economy, although that is its focal point and its most evident feature. We have to look beyond the economy. Globalization is primarily based on the elimination of technical obstacles, rather than economic ones. It is the abolition of distance and time. For example, it would have been impossible to consider the world as a single unit before it had been circumnavigated at the end of the fifteenth century. In the same way, I think that the revolutionary technological advances in transport and communication since the end of the Second World War have been responsible for allowing the economy to reach the levels of globalization already achieved. The starting point was the enormous acceleration and global spread of goods transport. In the past, goods' use was virtually restricted to the areas in which they were produced. And until recently, trade has always been affected in some ways by the inability to transport perishable goods over long distances while keeping them in their natural state. You could trade in grain, but not in fresh flowers.

The turning point was the appearance of modern airfreight. The simplest example, which we have all noticed, is the elimination of seasonal agricultural produce. Today, we can import tropical fruit, cherries, or strawberries irrespective of the seasons. Air transport has the necessary speed to bring them fresh to our tables. This has made it possible, for the first time in human history, to organize production, and not just trade, in a transnational manner. Until the seventies, a company that wanted to produce motorcars in a country other than the country of origin would have to build an entire factory and an entire production process on the spot; for example, in the Philippines. Now it is possible to decentralize the production of engines and other components, and then have them brought together wherever the company wants. For practical purposes, production is no longer organized within the political confines of the state where the parent company resides. Even this development would not have gone very far without the even more spectacular advances in information systems, which make it possible to control the process centrally and near-simultaneously.

Thus, while the global division of labor was once confined

to the exchange of products between particular regions, today it is possible to produce across the frontiers of states and continents. This is what the process is founded on. The abolition of trade barriers and liberalization of markets is, in my opinion, a secondary phenomenon. This is the real difference between the global economy before 1914 and today. Before the Great War, there was pan-global movement of capital, goods, and labor. But the emancipation of manufacturing and occasionally agricultural products from the territory in which they were produced was not yet possible. When people talked about Italian, British, or American industry, they meant not only industries owned by citizens of those countries, but also to something that took place almost entirely in Italy, Britain, or America, and was then traded with other countries. This is no longer the case. How can you say that a Ford is an American car, given that it is made of Japanese and European components, as well as parts manufactured in Detroit? It therefore seems to me unarguable that the global economy before 1914 was much more primitive. The one great factor that paradoxically made the economy more global in that period was freedom of movement of labor through mass migration. The interesting thing about the current phase of the global economy is that it has taken place under conditions of immigration control imposed by all the large capitalist countries.

However, in order to explain the distinction between appearance and reality, I think we need to return to what we mean by globalization, and what it wants to or can achieve. Suppose for a second what the most advanced stage of globalization would be like: a situation in which all the inhabitants of the globe would have the same access to goods and services anywhere in the world, assuming they had the same resources and the same money to spend. In other words, living in the Antarctic would be no more problematic than living in Rome or New York. Assuming that these goods and services could be produced in quantities to satisfy everyone's demand, the result would be that people would not be affected by their geographical situation. Well, it is nothing like that, primarily for practical reasons, because people have different resources, some are rich and others poor or their power is unequal, and some are free and others are in prison. This has nothing to do with the global dimension: it could happen within a single country or city, so it does not concern us for the purposes of our academic exercise. However, there are some products or services for which this absolute availability is impossible, even in a situation of complete globalization. Economists have studied these "positional goods," which by their very nature exist in limited availability or even in conditions of complete uniqueness. It is possible to guarantee that everyone can have the same access to Coca-Cola, but it is not possible that everyone can have the same access to a ticket to La Scala. By their very nature, tickets to La Scala are limited in number, and there is no way of producing more. Of course, you could resolve the problem in another way in practice; for example, by creating equal access for all to compact discs with recordings of the operas put on at La Scala. But this is not exactly the same thing, either theoretically or in reality.

Thus globalization, in a sense, means wider access, but not equal access, for everyone, even at its theoretically most advanced point. Similarly, natural resources are distributed in an unequal manner. The problem with globalization is its aspiration to guarantee a tendentially egalitarian access to products in a world that is naturally unequal and varied. There is a tension between two abstract concepts.

We try to find a common denominator accessible to all

people in the world, in order to obtain things that are not naturally accessible to everyone. The common denominator is money; that is, another abstract concept. At the same time, the technical process of globalization requires a high degree of standardization and homogenization. One of the great problems of the twenty-first century will be finding out where the tolerable limits of this homogeneity are, beyond which they would produce a backlash, and to what extent this process could be combined with the world's variety. Technologically, the trend toward homogenization is extremely powerful. Think, for example, of transport. When landing in some major airport of the world, it is already almost impossible to tell in what country, or even continent, we are in. The operational mechanisms have been standardized, are organized globally, and use the same language, English. A serious aircraft accident occurred recently because the Kazakh pilot was unable to understand an order in English, which came from the Delhi control tower. Send a photographer to the interiors of all the great airports in the world, and then try to distinguish the photographs: everywhere there will be the same shops, the same information icons, and the same colorful crowd. There is air-conditioning everywhere, so you don't even notice the difference in climate. In the same way, the procedures for industrial production are increasingly standardized, as are those for agricultural production. Thus, in my opinion, the problem in 2000 will consist of ascertaining how strong the obstacle to this growing homogenization will be.

*One of the innovations you referred to was the spread of information technology and communications in real time. According to Samuel Brittan, on the other hand, the Internet is not much more important than the invention of the transatlantic cable, which rapidly transmitted the news of financial collapse in Vienna to the New York Stock Exchange in 1873. What is the real significance of new technology in the global economy?*

We know that these things have transformed the international financial markets, creating a complete imbalance between the world's real economy, the production of goods and real services, and the flood of derivatives, rights, bets, and financial transactions that run through the dealers' computers. The sums exchanged in these financial dealings are many times greater than the world's total real product. This is clearly due to information technology, which makes all this incredibly easy. It even makes it possible for ordinary people, such as the so-called day traders, to enter the market by buying and selling with promises to pay, without the basis of any real money.

*Are we then at the threshold of an era of "democratic capitalism," in which large corporations and the heads of households alike will take part in the feast and share out the profits?*

This is the case in the United States, but this has very little to do with globalization. You are asking to what degree the ordinary citizens of the world can share in the incredible increase in global wealth, which still continues. What are the ways in which this could occur? The American way consists of constantly expanding the personal ownership of shares, particularly shares in companies that are thought to have a great future, such as those which operate on the Internet. These are companies that, as you know, do not yet make actual profits, but it is hoped that one day they will do so. The efficiency of this system is still subject to considerable debate. There are people in America who argue that this is a permanent solution to the problems of wealth redistribution. It is not clear to me how many Americans actually benefit from this division of the proceeds of national or global growth. Besides, it is also true that, outside the United States, this is not a very important factor in the economy.

One thing is clear, however. This "democratization of capitalism" has made enormous strides in the USA in recent years—the investing public is incomparably larger than it was in the days of what was then regarded as mass interest in the stock exchange. This has happened in two ways: by individuals entering the equity market, and through collective investors, such as pension funds, which is probably more important in the long run. It might be argued that, by investing money for people who wouldn't necessarily do it privately, such funds could become a really important democratic element in the distribution of wealth. At the same time, it seems clear that corporate or large investors have gained ground against small investors. In Britain, private investors are relatively less important than they were twenty years ago, even though Mrs. Thatcher's government made a massive effort to turn Britain into a nation of shareowners. Shareownership is now more unbalanced. This is another way of saying that the growth of the national and global economies is very unevenly distributed. The cake becomes larger, but the rich are taking an exponentially growing share of it.

*Globalization is often used by governments to proclaim their impotence and deny all responsibility in the management of the economy and control of markets. Tony Blair, whom you*

*have defined, a little unkindly in my opinion, as a "Thatcher
in trousers," is particularly assiduous in maintaining this
theory. It this really the case? Have states really lost all their
prerogatives? The German political scientist Ulrich Beck
speaks of "jubilant public suicide" committed by politicians
who exalt the market.*

I believe that this reflects a certain confusion between two
different things. Globalization is undoubtedly irreversible
and in some ways independent of government action. Not so
the ideology based on globalization, the neoliberal, free-
market ideology, or what has been called "free-market fundamentalism." That is quite another matter. This ideology
is based on the assumption that the free market maximizes
growth and wealth in the world, and optimizes the distribution of that increment. All attempts to control and regulate
the market must therefore have negative results, because
they reduce the accumulation of profit from capital, and
therefore obstruct the maximization of the growth rate.

In my opinion, there has never been any justification for
this view. You could perhaps say that a free capitalist market
produces a higher rate of growth than any other system, but
you would still have to question whether the distribution of
this wealth was optimal. As far as a free global market is
concerned, all that matters is the total wealth produced and
economic growth, without any reference to the way in
which it is distributed. Free-market economists wouldn't see
anything wrong if, for instance, you could prove that a completely free market could produce an exceptional rate of
growth in film production that would be much higher than
any other system, but at the same time, all films would be
produced exclusively in Hollywood and nowhere else. In
short, the free market assumes that the existing distribution

of advantages will remain unchanged, and cannot be improved upon.

A hundred and fifty years ago, the free-market theoreticians, who at that time were British, told the Germans that the best policy was to increase their agricultural production, sell the produce to the British, and import manufactured goods from Great Britain, since they could produce fruit and foodstuffs more cheaply than the British, and the British could produce industrial goods at a lower cost than the Germans. If this policy, which they thought would be the ideal arrangement, had really been pursued, it would have created highly unbalanced economic development. However, this is irrelevant to neoliberal theorists.

Besides, the argument that resources are distributed in an optimal manner by maximum capitalist growth has never been convincing. Even Adam Smith believed that there were some things that the market could not or should not do. So governments that adopt the ideology of the free market are not saying the same thing as those, including myself, who admit that globalization is irreversible. There are many ways in which globalization could proceed, without restricting itself purely to the removal of all obstacles to profit. If you look for the historical reasons for a balanced evolution of industry worldwide, you find that it was not produced by free trade, but by its opposite. The United States and Germany became industrialized countries in the nineteenth century precisely because they did not accept free trade and insisted on protecting their industries until they were ready to compete with the dominant economy, which at that time was Britain. In the twentieth century, the massive development of industry in the Third World was again protectionist. With the exception of Hong Kong, the Asian Tigers have been protectionist. Even the industrialization of countries like Brazil and Mexico was achieved by not accepting the logic of the free market.

Currently, there are very few governments that do not accept this logic. The ideological fashion of the free market is in some ways a by-product of the final phase of the Short Century: the break with the so-called Golden Age of Keynesianism. However, this fashion is rapidly coming to an end, if it hasn't already done so. When historians in fifty years' time look back on our era, they will probably say that the last part of the short twentieth century ended with two things: the collapse of the Soviet Union, and also the bankruptcy of free-market fundamentalism, which dominated government policies from the end of the Golden Age. The global crisis of 1997–98 may very well be taken as the turning point.

*The neoclassical economic theory of Von Hayek and Milton Friedman has now been widely criticized even by well-known speculators like George Soros, or free-market economists like Krugman and Bhagwati.*

Yes, this ideology is in crisis. Not only and not principally because it produced an imbalance in the distribution of wealth, but fundamentally because the system crashed. What occurred in 1997–98 seems to me to have been a significant breakdown in the global capitalist economy. It is widely held that the breakdown occurred mainly because of the lack of control over investment procedures and the flow of international finance. It is since then, and only since then, that the rejection of free-market fundamentalism has begun to spread. In some ways, it was dramatized not only and not especially by the crisis in the Far East, but by the Russian disaster. Intelligent capitalists started to realize this fact fairly early. Soros developed his critique of the free market from the beginning of 1996, before the boom gave way to collapse in half the world, and even took the American economy to the brink of disaster. You will remember that it was only thanks to the specific intervention of the American government and the Federal Reserve that the Long-Term Capital Management Investment Fund was saved, and with it the stability of the American financial system.

In *The Age of Extremes*, I suggest that we are moving toward a massive global expansion. The globalization of industry is making this possible. No one expects a final crisis of capitalism or a global catastrophe. Nevertheless, who can doubt that this was a major crisis? In the West, we have underestimated its gravity. As we all talk about globalization, we must see that crisis in global terms, and not just judge the effects that it has had on Italians or Americans. In global terms, it was dramatic. There are countries in Southeast Asia where it has been as serious as in America after 1929. Has that crisis been overcome? If so, this does not mean that we should return to a completely uncritical belief in expansion without controls. I notice that, in spite of the free-market rhetoric, we are now witnessing a return to protectionism and related disputes between the United States and the European Union, and also between the United States and China. It is very significant that these conflicts represent the reversal of the United States's free-market policy since the war. I don't believe that there has been a confrontation since the thirties between the United States and European countries of the kind we are seeing at the moment, with threats of trade wars and punitive tariffs. I would point out that this is something new in the global economy, particularly for the United States, which you would expect to back free trade 100 percent.

*However, it is impossible to underestimate how much wealth and employment globalization has brought the great mass of people who were previously poor and desperate. We are shocked about child labor in the Third World, but we often forget that, before, those children did not even get that miserable income, which today their exploitation makes possible.*

Of course, the profound change which globalization has brought into peoples' lives will have an enormous influence in the coming century. I do not only mean in terms of technological innovations, whose revolutionary nature is evident, but also in simpler terms, such as the mobility of people. Take tourism and travel. In 1997, the number of nights spent abroad was 630 million. In statistical terms, this means one night for every nine human beings. The extent to which travel around the world can change the world is something that, in my opinion, we do not fully appreciate. Before the last war, the number of Americans who went to Central America (Mexico and the Caribbean) never exceeded 150,000 per annum. Less than those who visit Disneylands in a day. The startling movement of people, like products and information, is unprecedented. What are its limits? Perhaps they have not yet been reached, but there certainly will be limits, physical ones at the very least. You have this problem in Italy already. How many people can go to Florence or Venice in a year? The world has become enormously rich. The number of people who have the minimum resources for doing things that previously only the rich could do is incomparably greater than before.

*Let's look at the Russian case. You have written that it is per-*
*haps the only country in the world where the theory that the*
*only thing an economy needs is the free market has been tested*
*to destruction. What are the results? I recently read that in that*
*country the pensioners now live on monthly incomes of be-*
*tween ten and one hundred dollars, and that half of the money*
*in circulation is foreign. Victor Zaslavsky has pointed out that*
*you have some measure of the Russian problem if you consider*
*that seventeen million East Germans have needed 900 billion*
*dollars in aid to get them out of trouble.*

Russia is indeed a special case. In theory, economists believe
in the complete triumph of the free-market ideology, but in
practice no country has ever tried to go all the way down this
road, partly because of the political impediments. No country, not even the United States, has been able to permit free
immigration. Russia is thus the only actual case where it has
been decided, from one day to the next, to apply completely
the free-market logic of capitalism. The results have been a
total disaster. If you compare the positive effects of the collapse of the Soviet Union and its political system with the
negative ones, I would say that the latter are undoubtedly
the greater. This is certainly true for the majority of Russians. Many older Russians say they would prefer to return
to the seventies under Brezhnev. It says a great deal about
the Russian disaster that Russians can see the Brezhnev era
as a golden age.

The scale of the human catastrophe that has struck Russia
is something we simply don't understand in the West. It is
the complete reversal of historical trends: the life expectancy of men has dropped by ten years over the last decade,
and a large part of the economy has been reduced to subsistence agriculture. I don't believe there has been anything

comparable in the twentieth century. You might ask whether this is entirely due to the application of free-market rules. I believe it is, if for no other reason than that free-market rules, even if adapted, require a certain kind of society. If that kind of society does not exist, the result is a disaster.

Gorbachev's failure was predetermined.

The situation in Russia was almost without solution, because the one organization still standing and still functioning, the Communist Party, was also the biggest obstacle to reform. Nevertheless, the destruction of the one organization in Russian society that could have taken some action, which is what Gorbachev did, virtually destroyed the Soviet Union. Indeed, Russia has condemned him. Compare Russia and China. For both these socialist economies, it has been clear since the sixties that, if they wanted to continue to exist, they would have to introduce elements of the market and take account of consumer demands. Since the sixties, Hungary, Czechoslovakia, and Russia itself had all attempted reforms that tended essentially in this direction. It was clearly the path to take. Whether this would have been compatible with maintaining the structure of the socialist state is another question.

However, if we compare China with the communist states where the regime collapsed following the end of the Soviet Union, it is evident not only that China has not collapsed, but that it has pursued a systematic process of economic reform in the direction of the market economy. They did this successfully, in spite of the serious economic and social problems, principally because the state and party did not abdicate their responsibilities. They had seen what had happened in the Soviet Union and they did everything they could to avoid it. This, in my opinion, is the real significance of Tiananmen Square. Moreover, they were perfectly aware of the need to organize the transition. That is to say that one cannot simply abandon the inefficient parts of the economy to the free market, but must also provide in some way for the future of the great state industries. You cannot just close them because they don't make a profit. As China has managed to maintain control over this process, the state has been able, in one way or another, to take responsibility for tackling the problems of transition. Ten years after Tiananmen, that country has a powerful, growing economy, and in many ways a rather formidable economy. Obviously, it has serious problems, but nothing even faintly comparable with the current state of the former USSR.

*There are many contradictions in terms in the laissez-faire school. Goods and capital circulate freely in developed countries, but not the labor force. In an economy based on competition, there is a proliferation of large-scale mergers in the attempt to create monopolistic positions in the market. While neoclassical theory talks of a "natural rate of unemployment" to be maintained in order to avoid inflation, today governments are emphasizing the fight against deflation and public support for employment. What is the bearing of this on the process of globalization?*

What is more natural than that an economy based on competition tends toward monopoly? That was the essence of Marx's analysis. Capitalist competition leads to capital concentration. In current conditions, this occurs more rapidly, but it has always happened. It really doesn't surprise me at all.

Many ideologues and politicians tend to behave as though

this process were uncontrollable, as though no government had the power to resist. They simply have to comply with it, and adapt themselves to its reality. This process has limits which cannot be overcome, and are essentially due to the political resistance of the populations concerned, as in the case of the limits placed on the immigration of cheap labor. From the point of view of free-market logic, there should be completely free movement of all production factors. Yet it has proved almost impossible to ensure the completely free movement of one production factor; namely, labor. For political and practical reasons, and in spite of all the talk of flexible labor markets, no government seriously believes that they should pursue such a policy by reducing Italian or British wage levels to the Cambodian or Chinese ones, because the political and social effects would be intolerable, or at least they are considered such.

The idea that globalization is uncontrollable is mistaken. We know it could be controlled. Although some things are more difficult to control, we know that control is sometimes possible simply because governments have sometimes done so successfully. Today, there is less free movement of labor than there was in the world before 1914, when there was no limit on immigration into either the United States or South America. No country, as far as I know, now has a similar immigration policy: not the United States, and still less the European Union, which in global terms is a mechanism for preventing immigration.

This brings us back to the great question of the conflict between the forces of capitalism, which are in favor of removing all obstacles, and political forces, which basically operate through nation-states and are either obliged or deliberately choose to regulate these procedures. This is a conflict because the laws of capitalist development are simple: maximize expansion, profit, and the increase of capital. However, the priorities of governments and peoples organized into societies are different by their very nature, and to some extent they are in conflict.

*You have called for some form of control on financial markets, and you are not alone in this. This control is supposed to dampen down irrational and domino-effect reactions which can transform part of the world into a gigantic financial crash of global proportions, in the flicker of an eyelid. But who is supposed to impose these rules? The nation-states which don't have the power? Or the international organizations which don't have the power and occasionally apply remedies that are worse than the problem they were supposed to solve?*

The international organizations we have only exist by permission of the nation-states. They have no independent power, other than that granted to them by the leading states; namely, the United States and a couple of other powers. Since the Great Depression, and particularly since the Second World War, there have been international organizations devoted to controlling the flow of capital: the Bank for International Settlements, which has existed since 1929, the International Monetary Fund, and the World Bank, which originate from the Bretton Woods Agreement, itself the result of cooperation between Keynes and American economists (probably it would have gone better if Keynes had been more successful, but that's how it went). However, these institutions are also dependent on the nation-states, so in reality, states are the only political authority. As we have already discussed, there isn't a natural tendency toward a globalization of political organizations, comparable with the economy's natural tendency to globalization. The two things are very different.

Whether an international authority can exist depends on a political decision and not on the logic of economic or technological development. This is a problem that will dominate developments in the twenty-first century. In the last twenty years, during the high tide of the fashion for market fundamentalism, there was a moment when it seemed that the states could be seriously weakened or even eliminated as obstacles to the transnational economy. There were discussions on the Multilateral Agreement on Investment, which would have given corporations the unilateral right to sue any state for any policies that damaged their profits. After a few months, the negotiations, which had barely commenced, were already dead. Moreover, I don't think that there will be any attempt to resurrect it, at least not in the same terms. Hence there is a constant conflict, and there always will be. It would be interesting to speculate on how the world would be if states ceased to be a limit on the development of transnational capitalist economy. It has been done by imagining a planet in which the basic units were no longer states, but corporations. Theoretically, it is possible to conceive a world no longer divided geographically, but on the basis of the two hundred largest international enterprises surrounded by smaller economic entities that still had the strength to be international, such as Benetton, and lastly a vast number of very small companies with access to global markets through the Internet, like that small family delicatessen in Britain that sells its products in every continent.

What would such a world be like? We know that the leading nations, the United States, England, France, and Germany, have been around for two or three hundred years, more or less as great powers. We know that they can become less stable, as we have seen in the case of Russia. We know that they could fragment in the future, like the United Kingdom. Yet the relative stability of the political map of the developed world underwritten by states is something that we can accept as an established reality. It is not clear to what extent this would be true of a world organized around the great protagonists of the global economy, such as GM, Ford, IBM, and Microsoft. Each of these giants could undergo changes in their structure that would be much more far-reaching than the ones that could occur in states. In the late Middle Ages, the Duchy of Burgundy was a great political and cultural power, and then it just disappeared. It is not inconceivable that parts of the economic landscape which today we consider to be permanent, such as General Motors, could disappear or be absorbed within a brief period of forty to fifty years. This is because the dynamics of the global economy are such that the stability of its protagonists cannot be guaranteed. Take the example of Olivetti, which is certainly not richer than Telecom Italia, and yet it can attempt to take it over. This is what I mean by instability.

Now, suppose the relative stability of states disappears: the instability of a world organized along the lines of transnational economy would certainly increase as well. There is a constant tension between these two systems, which today coexist and must adapt to each other. For example, it is clear that the international economy is hindered by the need to bend to national legislation, and has consequently always developed its own parallel system of jurisprudence. It is an attempt to avoid subordination to local legal systems, for example, by establishing the principle of recourse to arbitration by independent bodies.

However, we are and will be for some time in a situation in which the players in the global economy have to conform to the laws and institutions of existing state systems. At least this is true in the major countries. This does not apply to the numerous small irrelevant political units that can be manipulated and controlled by the global economy, such as Liechtenstein and the tax havens. But you should remember that even a country like Malaysia was able to choose its own way of dealing with the 1998 crisis, of going against the suggestions of international banks that explained what could not be done. Clearly, you can only go so far in interfering with the sovereignty of states.

The problem is not therefore whether the governments can control the international corporations within their borders. The problem is one of global control. In a way, when global enterprises and governments come into conflict, the latter have to negotiate as though they were dealing with other states. Consider, for example, the cases of when Volkswagen withdrew from Valencia or when BMW closed an important factory in England. In those cases, the governments had to negotiate with those companies as though they were states. Naturally, the stronger the state, the more it can obtain, but it still has to negotiate.

To date, the only attempt to control the transnational economy globally has been carried out by setting up a consortium of states, as occurred in the European Union. How far this can be successful is a matter for discussion. No one doubts that it is possible, although technically difficult. For example, in an extreme case, it would ultimately be possible for the United States to interfere in the actual physical transfer of capital, by rendering inactive a considerable number of the satellites through which the financial system works.

The danger in the current situation is that leading countries, the USA, European Union and Japan, might only be driven to take effective measures in periods of crisis. When the crisis passes, the incentive to act also disappears. This is what is happening now. For a few months, at the end of autumn 1998, there was a general consensus on the need to reorganize the international control of financial transactions, and create a new Bretton Woods. Now the Americans say that there isn't really any need. Nevertheless, I believe that in the end a greater degree of control will be decided upon. How is another question. There are considerable differences of opinions between experts, and between the International Monetary Fund, the World Bank, and the Federal Reserve. The paradox is that America is not strong enough to impose a new economic order. In the forties, if the United States and Great Britain agreed on something, then it went ahead. Today, if America really wanted to restructure the world's financial system, it is not clear that it would be able to do so.

*You are a passionate supporter of what you have called the Keynesian Golden Age, which in the West followed the Second World War. You have pointed out that growth in developed countries was greater between 1960 and 1974 (an annual average of 4.9 percent) than in the years dominated by free-market theories (between 1990 and 1997, the average rate of growth was 2.15 percent). But do your really believe that it is possible to apply the Keynesian recipe to the economy of today? Mitterrand tried at the beginning of his long reign, and within two years he had to give in to capitalist orthodoxy. Lafontaine tried, and he lasted less than six months.*

No economic policies are always and universally valid. Clearly, Keynesian policy worked very well in the fifties and sixties, partly because of the political conditions. There was a climate in which governments wanted them to work, but there were also particular conditions that cannot be repeated. It was possible in that period to increase profits, salaries, and welfare without reducing growth or producing unmanageable inflation. I wouldn't say that you could resurrect that economic regime. It certainly would not be possible for medium-sized countries to apply an economic policy without reference to the global economy, unless they decide to cut themselves off from globalization. At the moment, this is very unlikely, although it is theoretically possible. We have had some extreme cases, such as Albania, which practically isolated itself from the rest of the world, but managed to survive until the collapse of communism. It certainly wasn't a good, efficient, or rich economy in which we would have liked to live. The people were very poor, but it was a functioning economy. It collapsed when the political system that kept the world out also collapsed. Only then did it cease to function. I am not saying that there is a real possibility that others will behave like this some time, but it is something that we cannot exclude.

In the future, some parts of the world could decide to embrace protectionism, which would not be desirable because it could restrict the world's rate of growth. However, it would not necessarily be a disaster for the countries that chose such a path. Governments are engaged in a period of democratic politics, in which the interests of ordinary people are predominant, and in which they ultimately have to do what the governed want. Even in the most radically free-market regimes, health, public services, and pensions are generally for the most part provided by the state. These seem to me to be the three major social demands that every government must deal with, and none of them can be guaranteed without a system at least partly organized by government. Even in the United States, for example, no government, whether Democrat or Republican, would dream of abolishing Medicare, which in reality is a welfare service providing free healthcare to all elderly Americans.

No government, not even a conservative one, has ever attempted to abolish the Welfare State. They have spent the same on welfare as socialist governments and perhaps even more. They attempted to make it less attractive and to discourage citizens from making use of it, but they have not been able to abolish it completely. Thus governments have to have an economic policy that does not depress wealth creation by private enterprise but at the same time must provide for the social demands of their populations. In Great Britain, we have had a great debate over the privatization of the pension system. Thatcher tried, but it became clear that there was no way in which individuals could provide themselves with an income in their old age without some assistance from the government, even if it were no more than a set of tax rebates on pension savings. The pension problem is now less serious for most Americans because of the enormous growth in Wall Street share values. But this is a unique case, which concerns 5 percent of the world population at the most.

*One of the great forces behind the American examples and the global economy is consumption. The boom in the nineties was based on the consumer choices of Americans, who had practically stopped saving and spent continuously or invested all they had in the share market. You have written that "we live in an era which Marie Antoinette would appreciate, because the majority of people can eat cake instead of bread." Isn't it a historical irony that it is precisely much-maligned consumer-ism that is holding the system up?*

I think it is something more than a historical irony. The growth of wealth is so enormous that it has in effect completely transformed the situation. The global economy's capacity to increase production, even with highly unequal distribution, has transformed the consumer market first in the United States, then in Australia and in Europe, but increasingly everywhere. We should not forget that, whatever yardstick is used, the majority of peoples are better off at the end of the twentieth century, in spite of the extraordinary catastrophes that have marked it. There are one or two exceptions, in which the situation has deteriorated, particularly in recent years in Africa and Russia. But overall, we have today three times the population there was at the start of the twentieth century, and all these people are physically stronger, taller, longer-living, and healthier. They suffer less hunger and famine, enjoy a higher income, and have an immeasurably greater access to goods and services, including those which guarantee greater opportunities in life, such as education. This is also true of poorer countries. After all, there hasn't been a famine in India since 1943. Hunger in most of the world, with a couple of exceptions, is no longer something that human beings are obliged to live with.

This means that, for the first time, production can be geared to the demands of the mass of the population. In developed countries, human beings no longer live in the age of necessities, and can choose from the things they want, instead of having to choose between not having enough to eat and not having a roof over their heads. They no longer need to worry about their daily bread, and they only need to decide whether they want a sandwich with French bread or

cia, with cooked or smoked ham, and with fresh or
tomatoes. This has transformed the economy in terms
of services as well as material goods. Just consider the acces-
sibility of culture: the number of books and records, the
number of people who can find entertainment and information at all times of the day. There is no precedent for this in
the history of mankind. In developed countries, even the
poorest and the most abandoned live immeasurably better
than their grandparents did. This is one of the reasons for
the successful return of free-market beliefs, albeit only for a
short period. Its objective was not to abolish poverty or generate redistribution and social justice, but for all its injustice,
the poor tend to accept it, as even they are considerably
richer.

The growth in human production and in the availability
of wealth is enormous, and the greater part of the world
population has benefited from it. This is a feature of the
twentieth century that has to be taken into account when
making an assessment of what has been both the best and
the worst of centuries. It has killed more people than any
other century, but at its close, there are more people living,
and living better with greater hopes and opportunities. Let
us hope that the twenty-first century will experience further
progress, but without the catastrophes. But if there are catastrophes, they will be different, as a result of the twentieth
century.

*Another key aspect of the modern economy is the progressive
shift from the manufacturing industry to an economy based on
services. Many feel a certain nostalgia for the industrial
worker. Is the postindustrial society an excellent response to a
world in which ideas sell better than things? Today, industrial*

*investment no longer even guarantees an increase in the indus-*
*trial base, because of the new technologies. "More profits, less*
*jobs" is the credo of the new economy.*

This process has been accelerated by globalization, but isn't
necessarily an effect. Yet it is a mistake to talk of a postindustrial era, because in reality those goods and services that
were produced in the industrial era are still being produced
today. Although they are produced in greater quantities and
are more widely distributed, this occurs with a lower labor
input. The novelty of the situation is that, of all the factors of
production, the need for human beings is constantly dimin-
ishing. This is because, relatively speaking, they don't produce as much as they cost. Human beings were not created
for capitalism. This does not produce negative effects on
production, but only on human beings.

What I think we do have to find is another way to share
out the benefits of the wealth produced by a shrinking number of persons, who in the future could be very few indeed.
There are two ways of doing this. The first, the established
method of the past, has essentially been provided for people
by giving them a wage or salary in exchange for their labor.
For those who were not able to work, a transfer of income
was arranged that took from the person who generated income and gave to the person outside the labor market. Now
the number of nonworkers and incomeless has grown much
larger. We therefore find ourselves in the situation where we
have to find new methods of distributing national and international wealth. We also have to provide for some of
those who in the past would have earned their own income
in the labor market.

This is the biggest problem we are faced with. It is not a

question of increasing production, which we have successfully resolved. The real difficulty is how this wealth can be
distributed. The only effective method that we know is redistribution by the state and public authorities. This is why
I think the nation-state is still indispensable. Its economic
functions are perhaps less than before, but its redistributive
ones are more important than ever. I am not saying that the
state has to do it in its current form, but there must be some
sort of public authority that can ensure this redistribution.
What would happen if this did not occur? It is a question to
which the close of the twentieth century is already giving a
few indicators.

*The countries in the European Union, according to André
Gorz, have become richer over the last twenty years by around
50 to 70 percent. In spite of this, the EU now has twenty million
unemployed, fifty million poor, and five million homeless.*

It seems clear that only a small part of the wealth generated
has in fact been redistributed to the greater part of the population. The division of wealth is becoming dramatically less
equal. When I say dramatically, I mean that a very small
number of persons, often single individuals, are becoming
rich in a manner without precedent at least since the times
of feudal society, when the archbishop of Salzburg personally owned a third of the gross social product in the region in
which he lived. Since then, there has always been a certain
element of redistribution, which resulted in the truly rich
not being so rich. There were really very few people who
could compete with governments in terms of wealth. One
case of this kind was the Rothschild family, which at the end

of the Napoleonic Wars was as rich as countries like
and Great Britain. But it was an exceptional case.

Even billionaires like Carnegie and Rockefelle
were enormously rich, would not be so by today's standards.
I remember Rockefeller's famous line on the death of J. P.
Morgan, the great banker who was rich enough to create one
of the most extraordinary art collections in the world. He
left about $80 million, which in the twenties was a tidy sum
of money, and Rockefeller said, "We always thought he was
rich." Those great fortunes were smaller than the ones in-
dividually owned today by Bill Gates, George Soros, or Ted
Turner. I doubt, for example, that Carnegie, who perhaps
spent more on philanthropy than anyone else in his time,
would have been able to offer to pay part of the United
States's debt to the United Nations, as Ted Turner did. At
the same time, Soros, who spends his money on noble causes
at the same rate as Carnegie did, admits that all that he gives
away has little effect on his wealth.

The degree of wealth that is today available to individuals is absolutely incredible. Speaking in global terms, the
wealth in the hands of 1 percent of the world population is
immense. How will this affect politics? It is not clear. We
have signs from the United States that private individuals
can now manage to conduct presidential campaigns, or considerably influence them, with their private financial
means. Today, the rich are able to do what once could only
be done by large collective organizations. I am not sure
whether we fully understand the profound implications of
this phenomenon.

*Romano Prodi is the Italian who has been called upon to guide
Europe through one of its most delicate and critical phases. Do*

*you think that he has the ideas and the strength to carry out
this task? Where do you believe the process of European integration will end up?*

I don't know Prodi. I only know what I read about him in the
newspapers. I know that Prodi, like most Italians, is in favor
of a very ambitious Europeanist policy that will direct the
Union toward a kind of political federalism. It is not clear
whether this policy can be successful. It is obviously supported by the Brussels establishment, because that is where
the original idea was born. The extent to which the different
governments are willing to proceed in this direction is a
more complex question. It will obviously depend on the degree to which the large countries are ready to subordinate
their national sovereignty to the European project. I tend to
believe that there will be severe limitations on this path. I
think, for example, that the idea of a majority vote cannot be
extended beyond a certain range of questions, simply because leading member states—Great Britain and probably
France as well—will defend their right of veto over crucial
decisions. With the enlargement of the European Union, it
will be especially difficult for them to risk being put in a
minority.

Sooner or later, Europe will find itself in the situation of
the United Nations Security Council, where the countries
that are really capable of making decisions will simply not
want to give up their power to majorities. The power of veto
of the great powers was invented precisely for this reason, so
as to be certain that none of the great powers could ever be
beaten on the really important issues. This is why Europe
will grind to a halt on the crucial questions. It is extremely
difficult to determine a common foreign and defense policy,
and this proves that there aren't the necessary conditions for

an effective and total political integration, whereas there are for social and economic matters. The enlargement of the European Union will make the situation even more difficult: above all, you will increase the number of irresponsible votes. A majority made up of Slovenia, Estonia, Latvia, and a few other states of this kind could never be considered an adequate majority to be respected by Germany, France, Britain, or even Italy.

Another reason is that enlargement will have an immediate effect on national interests through the redistribution of resources. In theory, the Common Agricultural Policy will not be able to continue once the large and poor agricultural countries enter the Common Market, because the total amount of subsidies they would have to receive would become intolerable for the Union's budget. But the French, for historical and political reasons, do not want to reduce the social protection for their peasant electors. Therefore, I cannot see the possibility of progress toward European federalism without encountering sudden and serious international crises.

Equally, I do not think European integration can be accelerated by strengthening the powers of the parliament. The European Union was not founded as a democratic organization. I cannot even see the point of talking of its democratic deficit, because it wasn't supposed to be a democracy. Besides, if it had really been a democracy, it would never have reached its current degree of integration. The whole question blew up in the mid-seventies, when Europe became part of electoral politics, but up until then Europe was an affair that concerned only small groups of specialists. In theory, you could decide to turn the Union into a democratic government responsible to its citizens, but in practice I have strong doubts that the individual member states would be willing to allow this, with the exception of Italy. It is also very arguable that the European Parliament could ever have any real democratic credibility. Think about the low turnout for European elections, which, what is more, are invariably conducted on the basis of each country's internal politics.

Obviously, it's a good thing that the European Parliament is given greater powers, but I don't think that it will be able to take over the effective democratic representation of European citizens in the foreseeable future. For many Europeans, Europe is still a technical term, and not something to which they feel tied by any bond of loyalty. The question that people pose in relation to Europe is still always formulated in instrumental and domestic policy terms: how useful will it be?

There are only two important fields in which Europeans have already come close to each other and will continue to do so in the future. The first is European jurisprudence, which has already been established through the proceedings of the Court of Strasbourg. Governments have accepted that it takes precedence over their national laws. This means that, for the most part, the economic and social laws of individual countries have to be harmonized in their standards and interpretations. The other aspect that unites Europeans is, I fear, protectionism in order to resist competition from the United States and mass immigration from the Third World.

*Do you see the Franco-German engine of European unity as being in danger?*

It seems to me that France mainly perceived Europe as an attempt to affirm and defend its cultural and linguistic hegemony on the Continent. This battle was effectively lost when Europe was enlarged to include Finland, Sweden, and Austria, and French was replaced by English at press conferences in Brussels, because Scandinavians don't speak French. These things are much more important for the French than we normally realize. Europe, for them, needed to promote the role, culture, and language of France. Today, in my opinion, the French drive for European integration has abated. They have less interest in the process, now that their centrality has been visibly diminished. This is extremely traumatic for the French. Another obstacle is the deeply ingrained Atlanticism of the English. For everyone else, Europe is the only choice, while for the English there is always the possibility of a rapprochement and integration with the American system. Ultimately, the English have not yet decided. Of course, they no longer have a real chance of leaving Europe, having joined it twenty-five years ago. However, the alternative of combining both memberships is still open.

# 4) What's Left of the Left?

*What is left of the Left, or what has risen from the ashes? This is not just a theoretical question of ideas for a new reality, but also a practical one, given that the Left is in government in the majority of European countries, and even in America in its own way.*

There is a Left, because there is still a difference between Left and Right. Those who deny the existence of this division are generally on the Right. This distinction has a long historical tradition, which goes back to the French Revolution. It has certainly changed over the centuries, but we have to ask ourselves whether a division between the Left and the Right is inevitable, and therefore destined to continue, irrespective of the precise meaning we assign to it at different times. It is obviously possible to envisage politics that are not organized around these opposite poles, even though some kind of distinction between government and opposition is inherent in elective democracies, and therefore very difficult to eliminate, however much the differences of program might dwindle. I therefore think that we'll probably continue to have a political division that will almost certainly continue to express itself socially and ideologically along the dividing line between Left and Right.

However, I think the meaning of the term "Left" has

changed, particularly in recent decades. What hasn't changed, at least in developed countries, is the ideological basis that inspires all the manifestations of the Left, and refers back in various ways to the English Revolution, which was the basis of the American, the French, and ultimately the Russian Revolutions. The majority of the people who claim to be left wing still look back to one feature or other of this tradition and the ideologies associated with these upheavals. This is not necessarily the case in large parts of the Third World, but this bond is still effective in the West.

In general, the revolutionary tradition is not shared by the Right, although its more modern wing has internalized a part of it; for example, the concept of constitutional government. An attempt was made, especially during the Cold War, to divorce part of this tradition—that of modern liberalism—from the revolutionary tradition. This was mainly based on the argument that the tradition that derived from the revolution had led to communism and was therefore incompatible with modern liberties. France is a typical example of this attempt to break the continuity of the Left's tradition, the very feeling of being a family unit that held the *gauche* together. However, it does not appear to me that this attempt was particularly successful, especially after the Soviet Union disappeared. This gives a certain degree of ideological consistency to left-wing politics.

Of course, there have been various phases in the Left-Right distinction. Initially, the Left fought to overcome monarchical, absolutist, and aristocratic governments in favor of the bourgeois institutions of liberal and constitutional government. It was therefore a moderate Left, but was also willing to mobilize the masses for its political objectives. From the beginning of its history, the Left has been ready to be revolutionary. Take the Whigs in England: they formed a liberal party by entering alliances with middle-class radicals rather than with other aristocrats. During the French Revolution, powerful Whigs—dukes and owners of country houses—supported the risings across the Channel, just as they were to sympathize with Napoleon. For most of the nineteenth century, the division was thus between a party of change and a party of stability, or in more specific terms, between the party of progress and the party of order. The Left was on the side of change, and favorable to political and social transformations. Indeed, we still use this terminology: people on the Left continue today to call themselves "progressive."

Changes in the class structure gradually undermined some of this unity. The old ruling aristocracy was replaced or joined in power by a new ruling bourgeoisie, which did not oppose a certain degree of radical change. Thus in the twentieth century, and even more clearly in its second half, the nature of conservatism changed. It ceased to be simply the party of order and stability, and it took on new features. There are still remnants of that dislike of change, particularly those introduced by the French Revolution (the Roman Catholic Church is the best example). But there are fewer and fewer reactionaries in the nineteenth-century sense, people who want to turn the clock of history backward. I doubt whether even Pope John Paul II believes that today we can simply return to the past. A very strong current of conservatism favorable to very radical social changes emerged most notably in the seventies. Neoliberalism in economics and in politics is a new phenomenon in the latter part of this century. People like Thatcher or Reagan are genuinely right wing in every way, yet at the same time they propose radical innovations combined with more traditional right-wing convictions: patriotism, elitism, et cetera.

However, the last twenty or thirty years have been extremely important, perhaps even more important, for developments on the Left. Indeed, a new current has emerged, which effectively is a conservative one, because it wishes to maintain the status quo, when it doesn't actually want to turn back the clock. Take the case of the Greens: on the whole, politically they have to be considered a left-wing movement. Yet there can be no doubt that this current wishes to halt economic and technological changes, or at least to control them. In other words, it wishes to impose a suspension of progress. Thus we find a curious combination on the Left, which is evident in Germany, of traditional progressives with forces that believe in new agendas, which are not progressive in the literal sense of the term. So the traditional difference between party of order and stability and party of change and progress can no longer be used.

What dominates the second phase of the Left in the nineteenth century is the choice between the masses and the ruling classes, and the choice was for the class struggle. The poorer layers of the population, manual workers, organized themselves into movement, sometimes in alliance with the traditional Left, but increasingly on their own. This Left still exists in most European countries in the twentieth century. It was formed around the workers' movement and workers' socialist parties. These movements had three objectives:

1. They accepted the achievements of the old liberal Left (constitutional governments, civil rights, and rights of citizenship) and made them their own.
2. They fought for political democracy and the participation in and domination of politics by the great mass of the people. It is too often forgotten

how relatively young political democracy is. Hardly any countries enjoyed it before the end of the nineteenth century. The workers' movement was the major force in democratization. The right to vote was the only platform on which social-democratic parties ever organized general strikes. The situation was very different in America, because democracy came earlier and, unlike Europe, the Left never developed an independent working-class movement.

3. The new Left fought for the right of everyone to earn a living, for economic prosperity and social rights.

The combination of demands for civil, political, and social rights was typical of this particular phase of the Left, and was mainly supported by the working-class movements. This did not necessarily break the unity of the Left. In some countries, this unity from the moderate and liberal center of the political spectrum to the extreme Left remained a continuum. In the United States, this new phase of the Left remained within the Democratic Party, and in Great Britain labor continued its alliance with the Liberal Party at least until the First World War. It was the Russian Revolution that destroyed this traditional unity, by dividing the Left into two currents.

*What then happened to this second Left, which remained united until the storming of the Winter Palace?*

Many of its objectives were achieved after the First World War. Democracy and universal suffrage were implemented, although rather more slowly for women than for men. Some social rights and welfare measures were also introduced, sometimes with astonishing speed. Remember that the main demand for which the workers organized their annual May Day demonstration from 1890, namely, the eight-hour day, was introduced in most of Europe after 1918, at least on paper.

After the Second World War, of course, material conditions and welfare systems improved dramatically. In 1890, the words of the *Internationale* still had a literal meaning, but after 1960 it became increasingly impossible to believe that the "starvelings" who were to "rise" were really starving. This made a difference.

The Left's very success seriously weakened its program. Within this new Left, socialism was central to the aspiration of most working-class movements. It envisaged a radical change, the end of capitalism and its replacement by a completely different society. With hindsight, one might say that socialism was either a utopian dream or little more than an agitational slogan, for until the Russian Revolution not even the Socialist Left had really thought about what to do in the event of victory. There was not even a serious debate on how an economy should be socialized. It was generally accepted that it could be managed by the state on the basis of the model provided by capitalism of the time, in which the larger businesses were already in the hands of public organizations. Socialist theory was a critique of capitalist reality rather than a real project for the construction of a different society. And make no mistake about it, this also applied to Marxists. After the First World War, there was for the first time a real need to discuss the economics of nationalization in Germany and Austria, which in 1919–20 were on their knees. Bourgeois experts were able to criticize socialists who proved to have no idea of how they should proceed. The only available idea the socialists had was how to operate a war economy, which is in fact what the Bolsheviks imitated.

During the war and following it, the socialist movement divided into the social-democratic wing, which in effect became a state-sustaining party of reform, and the revolutionary and communist wing. The moderates maintained the old objectives of the Left, and achieved most of them, particularly in Scandinavia. In practice, they achieved everything they had ever hoped of achieving in the period between 1945 and the mid-seventies, with the formation and triumph of the Welfare State. These movements were not especially or even at all committed to battles for the permanent change of society's structure, although in theory many social democrats, such as the British Labour leaders in 1945, hoped one day to achieve a different and socialist society.

They accepted a certain degree of state intervention in the economy, in terms of both management and ownership, but this in itself was not a socialist project. We should not forget that Keynes was a supporter of the Liberal Party throughout his life, and he undoubtedly perceived state intervention as an empirical and pragmatic policy. Curiously, it was Lenin who realized that nationalization of an industry is not in itself a revolutionary act. Railways and public utilities were in state or other public ownership in many countries that neither were nor ever wanted to be socialist. The social-democratic wing of the political Left kept faith with the idea of a post-capitalist society through an ill-defined belief that public ownership and management would in time develop into something more and something new. Only the Bolsheviks consciously set out to build a socialist society. It has to be said that the failure of this project became overwhelming and patently obvious, especially in the 1960s and without question in the 1970s.

What is more, the Bolshevik system proved incapable of reforming itself and collapsed into ruin. This failure also weakened the ideology of the social-democratic wing of the Left, and so did the changes in the world economy after 1973, the end of social democracy's golden age. The coup de grace came from the spread of neoliberal economic doctrines that criticized the weaknesses in the so-called corporatist economic policies of the fifties and sixties, partly because they were no longer successful. The advance of the globalized economy struck at the foundations of the social-democratic Left, because it undermined its ability to defend its social constituency within national borders through a redistributive fiscal policy, welfare, and macro-economic stimulation of full employment. The present intellectual crisis of the Left has its roots in the twin crisis of the Bolshevik/revolutionary and social-democratic branches of the Left.

I believe that this aspect is much more important than the changes in the nature of production, the decline of industrialization, the growth of high-tech industries, and so on, because the working-class base of this Left did not begin to decline until the seventies. Perhaps the decrease in the overall number of workers started earlier in the United States, in the sixties, but elsewhere in the West, the period between 1945 and 1970 experienced such economic growth that the number of workers grew or remained stable, in spite of technological innovations. Still, only in Great Britain, and perhaps in Belgium, were workers actually the majority of the population.

In the seventies, there was no reason why the Left shouldn't remain as powerful as before, as far as its social base was concerned. However, this Left underwent a serious crisis. I attribute this to the fact that it had achieved its objectives, and that the conditions of workers had been considerably improved. Consequently, it no longer had a suitable program. It could neither propose the construction of a different society, because there were no longer any available models for such a society, nor could it reform existing societies, given that the social-democratic wing could only propose the conservation of that which had already been achieved. Thus the second Left came to an end.

There has been a New Left since the sixties. The trouble is that it has neither the solid class base that was the foundation of the working-class Left, nor a strong electoral base. It does not even have a single project anymore. Several of the movements that consider themselves to be on the Left tend to be single-issue movements. The women's movement is an important example, because in theory it has an enormous base, and yet it has a very limited program, even on women's questions themselves. The environmental movement is another example. These movements belong to what could be called the Left continuum. For example, the Greens, even where they haven't developed into full-blown political movements, are linked to the Left if they are linked to anyone at all, such as their relations with the Democrats in the United States or Labour in Britain. Where they have developed into a separate political force, it is much more likely that they enter into alliances with social democrats than with the Right. But this third Left is not very important politically, and its profile has mainly been raised by the crisis of the traditional political Left.

*There is another aspect to the crisis of the Left: the decline of politics as a credible system for the transformation of society. Wherever we look in America or in Europe, we see much more apathy in relation to politics (in the sense of a lack of active participation, partly and simply the result of electoral affluence).*

There is something even deeper that has gravely weakened the Left. Economically, it concerns consumer society. Intellectually, it is the identification of freedom with individual choice, without reference to its social consequences. In this sense, there has been a rift with the shared traditional universe of the Left. In the past, it wasn't thought that fighting for individual freedom was incompatible with the struggle for collective emancipation. At the end of the twentieth century, it has become increasingly clear that there is a conflict between these two needs. The privatization of society and the weakening of a common social identity are hitting the social Left hard, because this Left fights for collective objectives and pursues social justice. This is a serious and much wider problem, because what made it possible for the Left to act in a collective manner also makes it possible for democratic politics to function. Democratic politics exists to the extent that it is possible to organize people and get them to act collectively.

It is becoming increasingly difficult for every political movement to mobilize people, not only on the Left. Private and selfish interests have seriously eroded left-wing values. A good example is the gradual disintegration in recent years of mutualism in Britain. Look at what is now happening to the building societies in this country: they were cooperative savings organizations, which came into being when poor workers couldn't save enough on their own as individuals, and had to organize themselves collectively. The benefits were enormous, and these structures took on a considerable economic significance. Today, these societies are being transformed one by one from cooperatives into normal private companies owned by shareholders who receive dividends. The reason why members accept this development and vote in favor of conversion into a bank or public limited company is the little bit of windfall money they are offered. Neither the management nor logic itself are in favor of this conversion. Undoubtedly, the benefits for borrowers would be much greater if these societies remained cooperatives, but often people cannot overcome the temptation to collect one or two thousand pounds, which might perhaps be used for a holiday. They give away something of great social value for an immediate and short-term profit.

It is becoming harder to involve people in collective action. So long as most people were poor, they responded to this call, because their only hope was through collective action. If they are beyond the threshold of need, they think they can obtain more by pursuing only their own private interest. Nevertheless, the two great pillars of the Left's tradition are still standing. Of the French Revolution's original triad of Liberty, Equality, and Fraternity, fraternity no longer counts for much, but liberty and equality are still with us. We know what we mean by liberty. In practical terms, I think that equality today means social services and redistribution implemented by governments. This is something that the free market cannot ensure. Even Thatcher's conservative heirs, who more than any other right-wing currents undertook radical social changes in the direction of the free market, are now drawing away from this credo, and acknowledge, for example, that health, education, and basic welfare for old people are principally tasks for the state and public organization.

*So contrary to Thatcher's famous assertion, there is something called "society?"*

Not only does society exist, as we already knew, but there is something that society wants that cannot be achieved exclusively through the pursuit of private interest. There are social goods that can only be provided collectively in the common interest. Note that not even during the Thatcher period did the British conservatives dare to proceed beyond a certain point in privatizing areas like health.

I don't think that any Left can perceive the market as an ideal society, because as we have seen, there are things that the market is incapable of doing. My opinion is that any form of left-wing politics, even a very moderate one, must say what Jospin said: we acknowledge that the market is an essential element in economics, and perhaps decisive for the purposes of wealth creation, but we cannot accept a free-market society. Yes to the market, but no to free-market society. Although I don't know Tony Blair's personal opinions, the Labour Government would in fact prefer to enact some form of redistribution, and it does all it can in that direction, within the limits imposed by the risk of losing its electoral support. Chancellor Gordon Brown's policy is undoubtedly an attempt at redistribution, albeit a very fainthearted one. You might object that this is not the way to get great results, but you cannot say either that it indicates a belief the free market will resolve everything.

Admittedly, one or two governments of the Left have completely accepted the policy of the free market. I am thinking for example of the Gonzales government in Spain, but even in these cases I don't think that it was followed in the same spirit as Thatcher or Reagan. They did it because they had to, because there was no other way at that time, or because changes introduced previously by others were irreversible. These were empirical decisions rather than ones based on principle. I don't know if this is the case with Blair. He seems a Thatcher in trousers more than anyone else in Europe today, even to the extent of apparently enjoying the role of war leader. On the other hand, I could envisage moderate left-wing currents that say to themselves: all right, for practical reasons there is not a lot we can do to be different from the Right so we'll just have to adapt. In my opinion, this is Clinton's reasoning. You see, Clinton might be criticized a great deal for saying one thing and doing another, but the very fact that Clinton speaks in a certain manner means that by instinct he identifies with the values of the traditional Left. This is why he has disappointed many Americans, many more than the British who have been disappointed by Blair. Blair was never part of the Labour tradition, and we knew it when he was elected, but when Clinton won the presidency he looked like a Democrat in the best traditions of the American Left.

*Even so, hasn't Clinton been "the emperor of the 1990s"?*

I don't believe that Clinton is really an important figure in the history of the twentieth century. Nor do I think that he is among the more significant American politicians in the latter part of the century. Reagan was much more important. Moreover, he was more successful in managing the media, and in fact he avoided the kind of crisis that has continually dogged Clinton. Here there is an important problem: that of the quality of leaders. There are not many of a high standard. Incidentally, if you had a poll on the most important figures of the twentieth century, not many politicians would appear in the list. In Britain, many would perhaps say Churchill, but apart from him, people would probably put down celebrities who either have achieved something important in their own professions or are just simply well known. If you are a great sports star in the United States, you are much more famous than a politician. There are, in fact, countries in which film stars have been chosen as leading political figures. This has happened in a couple of Indian states, but not yet in large states like Italy or Great Britain. Of course, there is the case of Reagan in the United States. No historian should underrate the significance of the Hollywood actor turned president.

There is another major problem for the next century: the succession of leaders in democratic countries, and the transfer of power from one generation to the next. In traditional societies, there were tried-and-tested mechanisms, the best known of which being hereditary. In monarchies, succession does not represent a problem. Even in nonmonarchical systems, we have, for example, in India, the practice by which an obvious successor is someone who is a close relation of the previous leader and therefore already enjoys an aura of power. In other cases, the leadership selection process took place through a political organization. This is a traditional form in democratic societies: the person appointed to the position of leader is selected by a process within the body politic, which may be more or less democratic. In other cases, selection is the expression of a body of parliamentarians. In some countries, the procedures for this selection are completely obscure, as in Mexico, where in practice the ex-president always manages to appoint his successor, but no one knows exactly how.

The problem arises when the leader is elected directly. In this case, his profile is chosen on a set of criteria that are not necessarily related to his ability to do the job. It is a serious problem, because the quality of a leader is very important. Take the case of Germany, and think about how important the quality of Adenauer's leadership was. In spite of his limitations, he demonstrated the ability to pull his country out of a very difficult situation. The social democratic leaders who succeeded him also had great political experience, as in the case of Brandt. These men tended to have large personalities, whether you agreed with them or not. The present generation of German social-democracy is finding out the cost of its difficulty in selecting a leader of the same stature.

Obviously, these problems are less serious in strong and stable countries. Ultimately, it does not matter much who is president of the United States: since 1865, seven presidents have been killed or forced to withdraw before the end of their terms, and they were replaced by persons not selected to run the country. Yet the history of America was not significantly changed by these traumas. In the United States, the rails along which the train of power runs are so stable that whoever is driving can do it without derailment. But in the Soviet Union, the quality of leadership could make a difference, and it certainly did.

*Then there is — or perhaps, after Chancellor Schroeder of Germany threw out his first finance minister, Oskar Lafontaine, I should say there was — a Left that aspires to a traditional concept of social redistribution: high taxation on work and enterprise, and high social expenditure. On this front, there are now only those forces that refer back to the communist tradition, and perhaps part of the SPD. Does this seem to you a realistic policy for the Left today? Lafontaine couldn't manage it.*

I think Lafontaine lost because the financial world was against him, both inside and outside Germany. One of the principal proofs of the existence of Right and Left is that the markets don't usually discriminate against right-wing governments in the way they do against left-wing ones. Indeed, one of the surprising aspects of New Labour in Great Britain is that it has been successful in its effort to convince the markets that it is no longer left wing. The market made it impossible for Mitterrand to continue the policies he initiated in the early eighties, and now Lafontaine has discovered its power. Right or wrong, that is how things are. I think that in this sense Lafontaine's policy wasn't realistic. The SPD's policy had to be closer to that of the Center-Left European governments, like Jospin's. Lafontaine was too far to the Left, even compared with Jospin.

*There is another tradition that you have defined as "social Christianity," a laissez-faire current with a Christian basis, which has had a decisive influence in building the European Union. In a word, the "Rhineland model," which is personified by the new president of the EU, Romano Prodi. However, the Rhineland model also appears to be in profound crisis (five million unemployed) even in the Rhineland, and for the Left it is not very flattering to end up putting trust in a kind of compassionate conservatism. Do you consider this tradition part of the European Left?*

I agree with you: to turn to the social-Christian tradition is a sign of the weakness of the traditional Left. We have already talked about this. It is not encouraging when the only person of global importance to condemn capitalism is the pope. Yet you should remember that the Labour Party, for example, was persuaded of the case for Europe by the fact that Europe, thanks to the strength of social Christianity, guaranteed minimum trade union rights when Thatcher's conservatism did not. If you like, this too is a sign of weakness. Still, I am inclined to look positively on the social-Christian tradition, such as it is.

*Left and Right have become indistinguishable. The only way to mark out a division in the politics of 2000 will be between progressives and conservatives. The former promote competition as the modern means to assert individual talent under conditions of equal access to the social contest. The latter wish to maintain the status quo of corporations and privileges, including those of working-class aristocracies and their trade unions. The former speak to the young, and the latter to the old and pensioners.*

There is an element of truth in this. A large part of the Left has, in effect, become a force that attempts to conserve what was good in the past, or at least to safeguard it from further changes or erosion. On the other hand, you cannot identify the Right solely with support for an uncontrolled competitive economy. You have notably underestimated the other elements that have shuffled the cards. For example, there is the problem of nationalism and patriotism, which no longer find themselves on one side or the other. Where I strongly disagree with you is on the question of young and old people.

While it is certainly easier to mobilize old people on the grounds of preserving social structures, I do not think that any politics are having a great effect on the young. The depoliticization of the young is one of the most noticeable and complicated problems of our times. It is not clear what the role of young people will be in the politics of the twenty-first century. I think that they will be very important in small vanguard groups of one kind or another, but not necessarily as the central force for social change, and certainly not in electoral terms. Middle-income families of working age will count most from an electoral point of view.

There is not a single socialist movement that has a real youth organization. Actually, there hardly ever was, even in the past. The mainstay of the communists and social democrats was not young people, but families of working age. This is why, in relation to the decline of this social structure, I have many doubts over the future of politics—not just left-wing politics, but any politics. The young can only be mobilized on specific questions, like lifestyles, the environment, and questions of emancipation such as gay rights or drugs: causes that are only marginally connected to politics.

*There is, however, a structural feature to the crisis of the traditional Left in Europe. It started a hundred years ago as a movement of industrial workers, and today it finds itself operating in a society in which the specific relevance of manual labor and direct employment is declining dramatically. How can the Left address the new expanding middle class and the ranks of freelance workers? Will the Left have to abandon the idea of a workers' democracy in favor of a consumers' democracy?*

Modern consumer society, by its nature, increasingly compels political structures to adapt to itself. Free-market theory effectively claims that there is no need for politics because the sovereignty of the consumer should prevail over everything else: the market is supposed to guarantee maximum choice for consumers, and allows them to satisfy all their needs and desires through that choice. This route bypasses the political process, and makes it a by-product or derivative of the market. This is the reason for the tremendous spread of occupations like public relations and spin doctoring, and the application to politics of systems such as the focus group, which are in fact modeled on market research. This undermines the function of citizenship. If consumers are able to achieve their aims by exercising their power of choice every day through the purchase of goods or the indication of their opinions to the mechanisms of media consultation, what exactly remains of citizenship? Is there still any need to mobilize groups of people for political objectives? This development destroys the very foundations of political procedures.

The establishment of a direct relationship between the lowest point in the system, the consumer, and the highest point, the political decision maker, does not leave any room for the essence of politics, that which Habermas has defined as the organization of the "public sphere" in which people form opinions and unite to achieve collective objectives. This, in other words, is everything that we have until now understood by politics in liberal and democratic societies. That is what worries me about the Blairite version of the modern Left, because to me Blair seems to have fully accepted the market research logic, more than any other leader of the Left.

There is obviously still room for mass mobilizations of a

different kind. For example, there is the possibility of dema-gogic and populist mobilizations around particular figures or celebrities who attract attention and enlist the emotions of great masses of people. The case of Princess Diana is an excellent example. It is also possible to attempt political mo-bilizations suited to free-market society, in the style of Ber-lusconi who organized his politics in the same manner as he mobilized supporters for his football club. This reality is pro-ducing a completely new political armory, which the old generation has no experience of. We are only beginning to understand how politics could be conducted in this new manner. But the real question is: is it still politics?

This isn't just producing effects on the Left, but it is hit-ting the Left harder, because the politics of the Right, the maintenance of the status quo, can carry on without too much collective action. In the old days, there was a well-known phenomenon in British politics: when someone stood in a local election and said, "I am not a party candidate, I am an independent, and I'm not interested in politicizing local government," everyone knew that he or she was a right-wing candidate. Depoliticizing politics, therefore, automati-cally weakens the Left's potential. Yet mass mobilizations still occur, and perhaps they will continue in the twenty-first century, but in new forms. Just as someone got it wrong by saying that history has ended, I wouldn't like to get it wrong by saying that politics has finished. Nevertheless, I believe that the depoliticization of the great mass of citizens is a serious danger, because it could lead to their mobilization completely outside the modus operandi of all kinds of demo-cratic politics.

We can see how dangerous this phenomenon is in demo-cratic countries like the United States, where less than half of those entitled to vote take part in important elections, and more recently in Scotland. We would have thought it impossible, twenty years ago, that only 60 percent of the citizens would vote in the first election for a Scottish parliament in three hundred years, an election supposed to realize the historical ambition of the people of that country. In the first elections in South Africa, people queued up for miles to get to the polling station. Elections in the West are increasingly events managed by minorities, which do not involve the majorities, at the cost of the integrity of the political process. In the United States, the extreme right of the Republican Party, primarily made up of fundamentalists, has a disproportionate influence in the choice of candidates solely because the process is based on primaries, in which the majority of electors registered as Republicans do not take part.

*A way out of this democratic crisis, which is often embraced by the New Left, is a kind of media populism, or plebiscitarianism, based on a Faustian pact with the media.*

It worries me because it is another element that bypasses the political process. If the mass of citizens counts, then politics must be a process of mobilization, even just a symbolic one, as in the act of leaving one's home to go vote. In many ways, the media system substitutes itself for that mobilization. In a sense, the media are Thatcherite, because they do not believe that society exists, but only individuals. They establish a direct relationship with each person, house by house.

Traditionally, the electoral process has required a collective mobilization of activists in order to reach the electors. Today, none of this is necessary anymore. Theoretically, it is perfectly possible for an individual leader to talk to everyone through the media. It is already technically possible to vote from your sitting room with your remote control. Yet the symbolic importance of the electoral process, which activates citizens, albeit only for a day, is in my opinion essential for keeping society together and giving it a sense of being a community with the rights and duties that that entails. I'm not saying that all this couldn't be replaced with something different, but it is really difficult for someone who was brought up in another political era to predict how. I fear that the more politics is depoliticized and privatized, the more the democratic process will be eroded. Politics is becoming something run by minorities and, as in Italy, it ends up being perceived as not very relevant to the real lives of people. This is not a good thing for the Left, or for public life.

# 5) Homo Globatus

*The cultural landscape, as well as the social and political ones, has changed in the last decade of the twentieth century: people change their domicile and country much more easily, they have continuous access to information on a planetary scale, and they have powers of consumption that their fathers would never have dreamed of. Are they happier?*

Whether people are happier is one of the most difficult questions to answer, not only for an historian, but also for a contemporary. The only thing we know is that what Jefferson called the "pursuit of happiness" is a general motivation of human beings, at least in modern times. But it is very difficult to judge how successful this aspiration is in reality. It seems clear to me that if people live at subsistence level, that is without the guarantee of the essential elements to life, such as foods, clothing, and shelter, then it means a great deal to get just above that level. They are made happy simply by living in a situation in which they need no longer fear hunger.

If you look at the first-generation immigrants to the United States, you will see that those people certainly believed that they had improved their lot to the extent that they never returned to their homelands. Therefore, the growth in global wealth brings, and almost certainly will bring, happiness to the poor. The cost of this happiness could be the loss of norms, value systems, rules, expectations, and lifestyles. However, we should remember that, even in developed countries, this was not a big problem until the last third of the twentieth century. It was only then that the traditional model by which people conducted their lives began to be seriously challenged for the first time. These changes haven't even really started for the majority of humanity in most of the world.

If you live above the subsistence level, things are very different. Even an increase in income or a wider range of enjoyments do not necessarily or automatically guarantee a sense of self-realization or satisfaction. In a world where people can live on cake rather than bread, you cannot escape the stress of envy and social comparison. If you are well-off in a dynamic society, you cannot avoid making comparisons with the wealth attained by others in your social group, even if you have achieved all your expectations. This obviously reduces happiness and increases insecurity.

The twentieth century has brought a considerable amount of social and professional mobility, and I think the twenty-first century will bring more. This occurs not just within a generation. The children are more educated, cultivated, and prosperous than their parents. The main reason for this has been the enormous increase in educational standards, from literacy levels to secondary and university education. The latter, in particular, is a recent phenomenon on its current scale, within the last three decades of the century. For the first time in history, the majority of the population will be able to read and write in the twenty-first century, and a very high percentage will have a university education. In Britain, they are planning for half the youth population to go to university in the next century. More than a third of young people are already enjoying this opportunity in developed countries. Does this make people happier? Without doubt, it does at the lower level. The achievement of literacy gives tremendous satisfaction. I have students in New York who are the children of South American Indians, whose parents didn't even know Spanish and made their way in their own country by learning a rudimentary Spanish and acquiring basic work skills such as driving a car. They made enormous sacrifices so that the next generation could get an education. I have to say that, from every point of view, these families, which are still not affluent, show all the signs of really enjoying a sense of achievement, because they have accomplished things their grandparents would have thought impossible. They have become people capable of choosing lifestyles other than the ones they seemed destined to follow. This undoubtedly makes them happy.

Another element that should be considered is the effect that the enormous catastrophes of the twentieth century have had on the people who lived through them. I would say that, paradoxically and almost schizophrenically, these produced positive psychological effects for those who were involved, whether they were civilians or military personnel. Clearly, this wasn't the case for the victims, for the enormous number of people who were expelled, uprooted, or even massacred, but it was for those who survived. There is little doubt, for example, that the physical suffering of the Russians during the last war, which was greater than any other people, was on the whole surpassed by a sense of satisfaction and pride at having been strong enough to endure and overcome it. This collective feeling in some way reinforced the community. In Northern Ireland, where there has been a quasi civil war for a long time, the population's standards of mental health are higher than in the rest of the

United Kingdom. Indeed, following the peace accords, there was a sudden rise in the cases of suicide and depression. On the other hand, a break with traditional values and models can undoubtedly cause unhappiness, and can be very painful: when you don't know what you have to do, where to go, and who you will be. It is no coincidence that psychotherapy, a twentieth-century profession, is particularly widespread in two communities typified by systematic mobility and great uncertainty: Jews and Americans. In both these cases, it is very common to turn to someone who can help in facing up to situations for which the past gives no indications or models.

Last, the recent and significant problem concerning happiness is old age. The old, who are an increasing percentage of the population of the developed world, are in an ambiguous situation. In many cases, they keep their faculties much longer than before. Many of them are more prosperous, less dependent on others, and therefore a wide section of the third age in developed countries is more satisfied, because it no longer has to take part in the rush to make a living. We all see the aging American tourists who can travel on holiday and live life as though age didn't constitute any handicap to enjoying oneself. In the past in traditional societies, either you died relatively young, or if you lived a long time, you were generally pretty strong and in good health. Today, because medicine and science allow us to lengthen our lives considerably, the number of people who are physically or mentally weak is much greater. This is the cause of great unhappiness, and it will be increasingly so, as life expectancy gradually grows. The extension of life beyond its biblical limits—the Bible put the life span of human beings at seventy years, and up until the seventies, the majority of people respected this limit—is flooding the world with eighty-year-olds and ninety-year-olds. From this point of view, a longer life is no guarantee of happiness.

What will the situation be in the twenty-first century? Overall, I believe that the vertical reduction in phenomena like endemic poverty, and the emancipation of humanity from the dominion of want, will have a positive effect on happiness.

*There has always been a tendency for elites from each nation to share a "world" or "global" culture. But today, we are faced with something quite new: a process for getting cultures to conform with each other on a planetary scale, the global spread of a mass popular culture. You have already pointed out that 90 percent of films seen in the world (with the not insignificant exception of India and Japan) are American productions. The same is true of rock music: all young people in the world listen to more or less the same music. Football is another glaring example: I am a fan of an Italian team in which there are barely two Italian players.*

The causes are partly technological and partly economic. Clearly, this century's inventions like photography, cinema, radio, television, and the mechanical reproduction of sound have had an enormous importance, further increased by more recent technological developments that continue to produce effects, particularly through miniaturization, which render these technologies portable and available everywhere. The spread of the Internet is also significant, because it makes a wide range of technologies available. However, we should remember that, currently at the end of the twentieth century, only a tiny minority, albeit a rapidly expanding one, has access to the Internet. For the moment, it is restricted to the United States and Europe, if for no other reason than that an essential precondition for access to the Internet is literacy and often a knowledge of the English language.

Then there is the economic aspect: the growth of a global market has made rapid communication possible, so that the same television program or the same film can be transmitted to the entire world at the same time. This has transformed live performances, such as football matches, into genuinely international entertainment, in which teams are no longer linked to a particular country and still less to an individual city. There is a global pool of players who are recruited and shifted around the whole world in a manner that in the past only occurred for opera stars and great conductors. There is nothing that illustrates globalization better than football in the last decade. There is, however, a difference between traditional nineteenth-century high culture and modern mass culture, leaving sport aside, as it is by its very nature highly standardized. Traditional culture spreads through a European model that has been adopted globally and therefore globalized: a concert program in Osaka, Chicago, or Johannesburg will present the same kind of repertoire: European classical music. This is not true of literature because of a very powerful limitation on globalization; namely, language difference. Even the nineteenth-century classics have never been globalized in the way that occurred for music and the visual arts. There are very few people outside Italy who really think in their heart of hearts that Dante was the greatest of poets, because they have never been able to read him. Only Russians and those who read Russian really think that Pushkin was one of the greatest poets who ever existed.

In popular culture, on the other hand, we are faced with widespread syncretism at the end of the twentieth century.

The most obvious example is popular music, the assimilation of various elements, such as black American, white country-and-western, Latin American, and recently even African and Indian cultures. In a word, everything. A combination of all the different musical traditions is traveling around the world. Global popular culture is the product of this readiness to mix different elements coming from different parts of the world. High culture does not share this propelling force. There is one last problem with the relationship between high and popular culture. It is that the latter is shared by everyone, including those who are familiar with high culture, but the opposite is not true. Even if you love Mozart, you will undoubtedly be familiar with rock music, and you will have heard and perhaps even enjoyed it. This is why the global icons come from popular culture. They might not even be strictly part of it, and they might even be inanimate objects. When Andy Warhol, one of the artists of this century most sensitive to the meaning of popular culture, invented the famous set of global icons, he chose Marilyn, Mao, Che Guevara, and a can of Campbell's soup. The simultaneous availability of these images on a planetary scale made this iconology possible. How permanent are they? Warhol himself thought the majority of these icons would be temporary. We can judge from the extraordinary global impact of figures like Diana. I suspect that in fifty years' time, the events surrounding her death will be an interesting footnote, rather than a chapter, in the history of popular culture in the twentieth century.

*Yet in spite of the spread of a mass global culture, there is clearly resistance and even a revival of local, regional, and national cultures. Why, in a world that speaks English, do the*

*Welsh, who have the good fortune to speak it, want to redis-*
*cover Welsh? Why do young Islamic girls in London want to*
*dress like their grandmothers when they go the mosque? Be-*
*sides, it seems that globalization itself cultivates diversity and*
*cultural differences as market opportunities which, although*
*directed at niche markets, are profitable nevertheless.*

I don't think it's a paradox. First, I don't see any convincing
signs that currently local cultures are reacting strongly
against globalization. There are some limited cases of this
kind, but not on a sufficiently large scale. What usually occurs in immigrant communities is an increasing assimilation by the West, while maintaining the original practices
and traditions of older generations. This is still my opinion.
The first generation of immigrants tends to adapt as much as
possible to the new society, but at the same time, it is obliged
to maintain a link with tradition, because all its associations
and experiences are still rooted in its society of provenance.
Their degree of assimilation is therefore comparatively minor. Their children tend to assimilate themselves much
more, and more rapidly. Young West Indians, Indians, or
Pakistanis in London do not even have the accent of their
original languages, and speak English exactly like their con-
temporaries, even though they might be militant Islamic
fundamentalists.

I believe that the prevailing trend is still toward assimilation, not as an ideal, but as a practice imposed by living in
a society different from the one of origin. Perhaps the third
generation starts to develop a reaction in favor of a return to
its roots, which is what the Americans discovered in the sixties, when a whole new vocabulary of multiculturalism
was invented, when young people did not want to be just
Americans, but black Americans, Greek Americans, or Italo-

Americans. The third generation of American Jews rediscovered religious orthodoxy. Yet I tend not to believe that this is a general reaction against globalization. It's true that ultraorthodox American Jews went to the West Bank, and modified some aspects of their religious practice, but in all other ways they continued to behave like American Jews. In other words, assimilation prevails or tends to prevail. The same is true of customs and dress. If you go to an immigrant community in a large multiethnic city, the number of persons who dress in a deliberately different manner, like the orthodox Jews, is a minority. This is also true in the Muslim diaspora: not even fundamentalists dress in the external symbols of fundamentalism.

In my opinion, more probable than a reaction against globalization is a kind of syncretic combination of cultures, as with kung fu films produced in Hong Kong, where there is a mixture of Western elements, traditional Chinese ones, and various other practices. In this way, a number of local variants of global culture develop and fuse, rather than clash with each other. The reaction against the uniformity of life in countries like the United States expresses itself instead through the creation of identity groups that promote particular lifestyles, often rather bizarre ones, as in the case of New Age travelers. These are an aggregate of individual reactions, rather than community or collective ones.

It is indeed clear that there must be some reaction, if only because the babel of languages in the world is an essential limitation on globalization, and the increase in education and literacy will render this problem particularly acute for the purposes of the world's uniformity. The idea that one day the entire world will speak English seems utopian to me; it is something that will not happen. Multilingualism, by definition, is an obstacle to globalization. We mustn't get confused: globalization, which is a real and widespread phenomenon, is quite different from cosmopolitanism, which is still extremely limited.

*Therefore, you don't agree with what the sociologist Anthony Giddens has written: "The clash between dependence on tradition and individual autonomy is one of the poles of globalization. At the other pole, there is a clash between cosmopolitanism and fundamentalism"? Giddens argues that fundamentalism is a child of globalization, because "no one would have any reason to live, if they didn't have something that was worth dying for."*

I don't believe that globalization has anything to do with fundamentalism, except for the fact that anything that upsets tradition has some effect on fundamentalism, and globalization is obviously one of these things. Indeed, the fundamentalist reaction is less common precisely in those countries that are more globalized. Fundamentalism is a reaction against everything that comes from the outside world. Whether or not it is globalized is of little consequence.

The question of whether there is still something worth dying for equally has nothing to do with globalization. It concerns the decline of collective values with the growth of a highly individualistic society. I think the extreme example was the war in Kosovo. It was carried out in the name of the highest moral values and, at the same time, on the basis that under no circumstance was a single NATO soldier to die. This principally concerns the United States, perhaps the only country in the world where they expect soldiers to kill without the risk of dying. But in a large part of the world, I don't think there is any lack of causes for which people are willing to die. Some—the good causes—have disappeared, but the bad ones are as strong as ever. The readiness with which Albanian emigrants rushed to Kosovo to join the guerrillas demonstrates that there are still many people willing to put their lives in real danger. The last example, following the end of the Cold War, of a large-scale conflict in which people were willing to die for a cause was the Iran-Iraq War. Besides, it is possible to foresee a war in the future between China and the United States that could induce Americans to accept the risk of battle just as their grandfathers and great-grandfathers did.

A long period of peace radicalizes behavior and divides people into two groups: one that is ready to run risks, not necessarily in the armed forces, and one that refuses to take them. For example, there are today an increasing number of people who practice extreme and dangerous sports, which involve a probability of losing one's life, and there are people who accept warfare as a paid professional activity. On the other hand, the lasting peace has created a large and placid majority in wealthy countries, for whom the idea of dying for a cause isn't a concept that they would ever contemplate. With the decline of general conscription, this attitude is destined to take root. It is not easy to imagine how this could change, or whether there could be a return to the reality of the twentieth century in which wars made every individual face up to the question of death, either at home under the bombs or at the front. Indeed, this type of war will not be common in the future.

This is true of the developed and pacified Western world. It does not mean that elsewhere there is any lack of people ready to die for a cause, because, to some extent, this is an inherent part of human nature.

*Many of the traditional bonds that tied an individual to his reality have been weakened by globalization: loyalty to one's family, village, neighborhood, and company. In America, young people who are starting out now on their working life must expect to change companies as many as ten times, and also their profession. Competition leads to tremendous psychological stress, and social envy afflicts the upper levels of society.*

Let's not mix up different things: globalization and the break with traditional lifestyles. The only aspect of this break that can be directly connected to globalization is insecurity of employment, because globalization is supposed to force companies to adopt greater flexibility in their workforces. But even this, in the majority of cases, is not due to international competition. Insecurity of employment is a new strategy and a tactic for increasing profits by reducing as much as possible the reliance on human labor or by paying employees less. In the modern capitalist economy, the only factor whose productivity cannot easily be increased and whose costs cannot easily be reduced is human beings. There is therefore enormous pressure to eliminate them from the production process. This would be true, whether or not there were global competition. It is more the case that this is the excuse by which this process is justified today. Only recently, an English bank decided to charge its customers five pounds every time they deal with counter staff in branches. They are doing this because in reality they don't want customers at the counters, they want to close branches, and they want customers to use automatic machines for all transactions: in short, they want to do without bank staff. This is an iron law of capitalist production in itself, rather than one of global competition. If automation makes it possible, banks will reduce their staff levels, irrespective of any competition from a bank in Hong Kong.

We must be able to make distinctions, but it is undoubtedly true that this will be one of the great problems of the twenty-first century. Today, we tend to accept as proven that we no longer need any of the traditional motivations that in the past not only kept human societies together, but also made the economy work. Motivations such as the family or the value of work. Adam Smith considered the motivation for the free-market economy to be not only the assumed psychological need to exchange goods, to buy and sell, but also man's typical tendency to work and his willingness postpone the immediate gratification of his labor. Without this attitude, many aspects of the market would not be able to function at all.

These foundations of our society have been completely disrupted by the economic, social, and cultural revolution of the latter part of the twentieth century.

It stuns me how little attention is paid to the fact that these effects could be disruptive for the efficient operation of the capitalist system itself. For example, the life of many companies was based in the past on a general acceptance of the values of solidarity and family bonds. This is still true of Italy and its small-business "miracle." It is still true of the lively and enterprising Chinese diaspora of Southeast Asia. Family solidarity in these cases provides a reliable supply of cadres, ready to share the company's interests, and for whom feelings of obligation and duty do not have to be imposed from outside, but are in some way inscribed in their moral codes. It seems to me today that, in this free-market era, the idea is gaining ground that these ancient motivations are no longer important, that they can be discarded without any consequences, and that an economy can be entirely managed without making any use of them. The loyalty of workers or management to their company is considered to be of no influence. It is believed to be perfectly possible for a company's successes to coexist with permanent insecurity and a continuous turnover of employees.

There are other features to this tendency. It is actually assumed that human beings are no longer willing to wait to obtain recompense for their labor or business enterprises, and that they demand immediate gratification. No one invests any longer to build a new company that will operate in ten years at the earliest, and will start to make profits after another ten. The only logic of investment that is now valid is that of participating in something that will produce an immediate premium. In fact, it is much more common to buy existing companies than establish new ones. In these glorious days of international speculative finance, people do not measure the result of their business activities at the end of a decade, and not even at the end of the year. The success of an investment is calculated day by day, and perhaps even hour by hour. The question is: for how long can capitalism operate with this particular economic modus operandi? For someone like me who comes from another generation, it is very difficult to give an answer. For many of us, the idea of not having any security about what will happen tomorrow is completely foreign and frightening. Perhaps it will be possible for future generations to adapt to this system and consider it normal, but if they succeed, it will be at the cost of enormous stress and terrific tension. I have no doubts about this. What isn't clear is whether this is sustainable over the long term.

There are activities that, in my opinion, cannot be organized in this manner at all, that is, on the basis of the maximum and immediate remuneration, or in other words, according to the rules of the competitive market. Science is one example. One of the things that causes me most anguish about the future is whether science, which has been one of the few things that has resisted this system's break with traditional values, will also be changed by the new reality. In America, scientists are among the few whose activity is not yet exclusively motivated by the expectancy of maximum profit. The danger of the biological and genetic revolution is that scientists understand how much money they could earn if they too adhered to this logic. Will they too be sucked into the system by which the financial market already works? If and when this happens, the consequences could be so important that today it is impossible even to attempt to imagine them. This could also be true of funding scientific research, which for the most part in the past has occurred without immediate reference to the profit and loss account. Some research, such as that carried out by CERN, has been pursued over years not for any immediate profit or military requirements, but because governments considered it as one of the aspects of international competition between states. But if the only criterion for international competition were maximum profits, would there be no more need for CERN?

I tend to think that this idolatry of market values will not last. It is a system that can work fine for some types of activity, such as speculative finance or the entertainment industry, but if you consider the great success stories of industrialization in the final part of the century (Japan, Korea, China), you will see that they were not at all based on the abolition of the bonds between company and workers. In fact, I think that at least for as long as humans are still necessary and haven't been completely eliminated from the production process, it will be almost impossible to eliminate the importance of their satisfaction and motivation, and therefore their collective feelings, such as loyalty to family, community, company, and state.

*The imperative of self-realization and removal of all suffering is giving rise to a new cosmetics of affluence. It is no longer enough to be healthy and rely upon an efficient health system. We also want to be sexually active past middle age, and we therefore need Viagra. We no longer want to experience sadness or listlessness, and so we turn to Prozac. We want to be thin with a flat stomach, and thus we get pills that dissolve fat or indulge in excessive dieting to the point of causing new social illnesses, such as anorexia and bulimia. Do you not think that we risk creating new forms of discrimination, no longer based on income, but on obesity, ugliness, timidity, or a lack of interest in sex?*

I think these are problems restricted to rich countries. I don't think they worry Tamils or Albanians very much. Nevertheless, it is a question worthy of discussion. The availability of these new treatments will depend on costs. The reason why people consider discrimination against certain types of patient, such as the overweight or smokers, in free medical treatments, is one of cost. A public health system must restrict the use of medicines like Viagra, as has happened in Great Britain. Besides, there are very few cases that would justify its free distribution on medical grounds. The problem is that, in democratic societies, the very fact that someone perceives a desire, such as the one to be more sexually potent, creates a right to medical treatment. There is therefore considerable pressure from public opinion.

Another good example is AIDS. For many years in the

United States, where it was not the most widely spread and serious health emergency, pressure groups that were concerned with the issue were very effective in attracting wide public attention and large amounts of resources. In social terms, there were many other evils that merited at least as much investment and research. Now that AIDS has truly become a mass health problem in Africa, the situation is different and interest is low, partly because there are no democratic societies and pressure groups in Africa.

However, the most important matter in reply to your question is the analysis of how social hierarchies are formed. We can predict with certainty that the richer the world becomes, the less equality there will be, including political and legal equality. The egalitarian systems in history, socialist regimes like Russia and Mao's China, were based on the fact that, being poor countries, there were no mechanisms working to produce a wealthy class. Of course, even in the Soviet Union, and to a lesser extent in China, there was a minority that was better off than the general population. Yet compared with the West, these standards of wealth were ridiculous. A dacha belonging to Stalin or a member of the soviet nomenklatura was a status symbol, but any relatively prosperous Milanese professional has a much more beautiful second home on Lake Como.

In the rich countries where the economy is practically unbridled, the variety of incomes is already enormous, and is going to grow further. How many dollar millionaires are there in Italy, France, or Great Britain? The number of persons whose total assets amount to or exceed a million dollars is extremely high even in Europe, even though growth is not at American levels. On the other hand, the advantages of great wealth are no longer so obvious, mainly because the available goods and services for everyone are so sophisticated and widespread that enjoyment of them no longer distinguishes the rich from the nonrich. When more than 90 percent of a population has a television, the advantage of having a giant high-definition screen is relatively less important than possession of a television was at the time when they were the privilege of the few. Thus even the symbols of wealth are changing. Today, the status symbol of the truly rich is a private plane. An American academic, whose work consisted of collecting donations for his university, once explained to me the secrets of his trade: "First, you have to like the rich. Second, you have to know what to talk to them about, and the subject that is certain to interest them is their private planes."

The really new feature of the distinction created by wealth is that the assets that define them today must be esoteric and exclusive. Only the rich know where they go on holiday, because they are the only people there. Yet one of the traditional bases of social hierarchy was that generally it could be seen, recognized, and appreciated by everyone. In this sense, wealth today gives less satisfaction. In the past, for instance, there was a considerable correlation between being rich and being healthy and good-looking. The English landowning ruling class were taller, stronger, and better looking. However, this distinction is also gradually fading. Nevertheless, I believe that wealth will remain pivotal in defining social hierarchy. I cannot see any alternative hierarchies emerging that could compete with the availability of money.

For a long time, the Church was an alternative hierarchy. The position of the pope still does not depend on how many private aircraft he owns, but secularization is also undermining social hierarchy based on the exercise of religious power. Politicians? They are educated men and women, and in the past education was a decisive factor in social hierarchy. They will probably continue to be higher up than others, but a rung lower than the rich. Artistic talent perhaps? It will definitely count for a great deal, partly because it can be translated in financial gains. Physical perfection? Well, sporting accomplishments have always been much appreciated. It is certainly true that from the sixteenth to the nineteenth century, sport was subject to the fashions of the aristocratic society in which it was born. People who were excited by the skills of jockeys or boxers lived in a culture predominantly organized by aristocratic society. Today, this has disappeared. Sport has also become a market activity. I don't think this has reduced the exceptional admiration aroused by great sporting achievements. Until quite recently this had nothing to do with how much money a sportsman made, and indeed for most of the century the great stars didn't make much anyway, at least outside the USA. Sporting success guarantees an extra authority in the definition of social hierarchy. It lifted Pele to such an exalted position that he became a minister. I don't think this factor will disappear. Indeed, it will concentrate on the individuals and their personal images, while neglecting their teams or countries of origin.

*In your opinion, have women come out of their war of liberation as victors or vanquished? Have they really attained equality with men? Is this equality the same thing as liberation, or is it perhaps a way of conforming to the male myths, power and sexuality?*

There can be no doubt that the emancipation of women has been one of the great historical events of the twentieth century. The problem for the twenty-first is to establish what still has to be done, and what will probably happen. In the twentieth century, the emancipation of women was, in fact, confined to a part of the world and certain section of society. There are still large parts of the globe where this phenomenon has not occurred. There have been two great phases: the first was the battle for the same political and voting rights, the second was for equality in access to the professions. Technically, these objectives have been reached since the end of the Second World War. By then, the countries in which women could not vote were a small minority, and then they disappeared. Women's progress in the professions had been enormously encouraged by the war, and in the last thirty years, by the increasing need of families to have two incomes instead of one. I think that the successes in the workplace have been satisfactory, although you could certainly say that it is not enough. Nevertheless, I think the spread of female employment is a quite spectacular phenomenon, particularly in countries like the United States and Great Britain.

There is, however, a serious problem, and it has become increasingly serious: the extraordinary difficulties for women of combining high professional posts with being mothers. This has nothing to do with discrimination, but with the natural law that women are the ones who give birth. It is theoretically possible to resolve the problem by entrusting children to baby-sitters, nursery schools, and letting people other than the natural mothers bring them up. History tells us that this is possible: the aristocracy practiced this on a vast scale. But today, everyone agrees that this is not the best solution for children. It is therefore a problem that is likely to carry an emotional and social cost for future generations. This explains why the percentage of women who reach the top of their professions is lower than that of men. For this reason, many women are simply not capable of competing beyond a certain point. Besides, it is wrong to assume that it is purely a statistical question to be resolved with quotas dividing every type of work equally between men and women. I see no historical reason why the ideal composition of a profession, such as Parliament, should be 50 percent women and 50 percent men. On the other hand, there has been a tendency in the past for a division of labor based on sex, which in some cases has been historically very ancient. For example, men went into the army and women went into obstetrics. On other occasions, it occurred for chance historical reasons, such as the feminization of the teaching professions and medical practice in the Soviet Union.

However, the sixties produced a great change, which had nothing to do with competition between the sexes: the control of procreation by women. It was a real historical event: a kind of declaration of women's independence from men, and to some extent from the rules that maintained the entire social community. A typical element was that women decided to no longer accept the teaching and moral authority of the Church, particularly in famously Catholic countries like Italy, Ireland, and Poland. It was a phenomenon that extended beyond the restricted circle of educated women who constituted the vanguard of the movement for equality. It had far-reaching consequences, because it transformed the entire mechanism for the reproduction of the human race, from one generation to the next. It allowed women to exercise the right not to have children. The speed with which it occurred was astonishing, and the consequences are still unpredictable.

Greater emancipation of women will be a feature of the twenty-first century. Its most effective weapon will be the spread of education around the whole of the planet, even in the most backward countries. This revolution will be propagated by the discovery that other people do things differently from what were considered the immutable laws of nature. From this point of view, the emancipation of women is only in its initial stages, because it has not yet addressed the majority of the world's population. In politics, on the other hand, the rise of women has curiously been a lot less satisfactory, because, even though women have become parliamentarians, ministers, or prime ministers in many countries, we cannot say that politics has been changed in any way or become more feminine.

*I would like to know your thoughts on the technological revolution. It is often interpreted as one of the most potent factors of democratization, because it brings information to every home and makes it possible to work outside the traditional production units, and is therefore more flexible in adapting to individual talents. Do you share this optimism?*

Information technology is certainly producing considerable changes in work. I am skeptical about the possibility of radical change, just as I am skeptical about the ability of the modern economy to operate without any kind of reference to social traditions. Obviously, it is technically possible to work from home and communicate with the world solely by e-mail. The reality is that this is not the way people want to work. Even the high-tech pioneers do not live scattered across the United States and Great Britain, but are concentrated in certain areas where they can meet and communicate. It is not very comforting for human beings not to have someone to speak to, and to renounce personal contacts. This is an absolutely essential element for productivity and efficiency at work. All this talk about decentralized domestic work is partly a good bit of propaganda to justify redundancies. British Telecom is preparing to free itself of 10 percent of its workforce on the assumption that they will be able to work from home. Besides, it is a case of technological utopianism that ignores the fact that human beings don't want to be on their own, but prefer to work with others.

In the field of work, socialization is and remains absolutely essential. We know that in the country people go to the market not only to buy things but also to meet other people and exchange news and gossip. You cannot build a society on the basis of cost-benefit ratios. But even from this point of view, it is much more efficient to have a Microsoft Research Center than to scatter your researchers from Canada to the Philippines. Silicon Valley is a typical example of how you reach the critical mass of labor necessary for operating even the most advanced of industries. Most people engaged in software jobs in India live in Bangalore. Even those who are most enthusiastic about the advantages of communicating over long distances prefer to meet each other at the same bars to find out how things are going and what is state-of-the-art. The same is true of universities. The first question that a good scientist will ask when a university offers him or her a place is how many other people are there with whom he or she can talk about their work.

*Doesn't the power of science frighten you? The possibilities of cloning human beings, crossing animal and vegetable genes in a tomato, or killing in war while sitting in front of a computer?*

Of course it frightens me, not only because of the immense power it confers, but also because the sorcerer's apprentice often doesn't know how to use it. If there was some guarantee that the persons who make these developments possible also knew what to do with them, how to use them, and when not to use them at all, I would be less frightened. But that guarantee does not exist. Immense natural forces are being manipulated and are not always perfectly understood. There is no regulation or institution that can say what to do and what not to do. The only rule that exists in free-market conditions, the maximization of economic growth and profit, will almost certainly produce negative effects.

# 6) 12 October 1999

*The 12th of October 1999 is the date on which the six-billionth human being will be born. To what extent will this child be able to live a dignified, productive and happy life?*

The inequality of opportunity in the world will be one of the crucial factors in the future of mankind, both as a collectivity and as individuals: regional inequalities, geographic inequalities within the same country and social inequalities. The great problem for the next millennium is that it is impossible to make general predictions on the future of child number six billion.

*How do you explain demographic trends in Europe, and the fact that zero or negative growth is becoming a typical feature of the developed world?*

This is true. This important phenomenon is not only occurring in the wealthy part of Europe, but also in Eastern Europe. There are many countries in the ex—Soviet Union and elsewhere, such as Hungary and Romania, where the population is already dropping. In the old Continent, the countries where renewal and modernization were obstructed by the Soviet program are the ones that are experiencing the worst situation.

Hence the fall in the birthrate is shared by extremely rich countries and ones that are quite the opposite. I think that the demographic disparities in the different regions of the world will ultimately be one of the greatest problems for the next century.

Let's first consider the point to which the overall world population has got: six billion. Demographers now predict that this growth will stabilize within the first half of the twenty-first century at around ten billion. The problem is that long-term demographic predictions have never turned out to be very accurate. The predicted stabilization is based on the assumption that the whole of the Third World, or at least the greater part of it, will repeat the demographic trends previously followed in the First World; namely, that it will experience a sudden and conspicuous drop in the birthrate, combined with a large increase in life expectancy. There are signs that this is happening, but all the same, we are dealing with a forecast based solely on experience and mathematical models. We must therefore be very cautious.

There have already been several attempts to predict population trends during the twentieth century. For example, it was widely speculated between the wars that there was going to be an imminent decline in the European population. Instead, we discovered the baby boom after the Second World War even in highly developed countries. What can be said with reasonable certainty is that if this predicted stabilization does not occur, then the current rates of growth in the world population will inevitably lead to a catastrophe of one kind or another. There must be a point beyond which it will produce massive negative effects on a global scale.

So we can only reason on the basis of this hoped for halt in growth. But even in this case, many questions remain unanswered. We don't know if this stabilization will follow past models, which partly involved changes in social behavior, such as marriage, and partly reflected deliberate interference in the reproductive process, such as birth control and abortion. I think that, if this stabilization occurs, it will be the product of a low birthrate and a low death rate at the same time. These two factors together can produce a particular age composition for a population. On the other hand, we don't have any experience of what long-term demographic stability really means. What I am saying is that not only do we not know how to achieve it, but we also don't know how to maintain it over long periods, ensuring that each generation is more or less of the same size as the previous one. Will there be fluctuations, dramatic ups and downs? We have to know this, if we want to know what will happen. But it is impossible to predict.

Still less do we know what will happen when, as is now occurring, part of the world stops reproducing and another part has a large surplus population, and therefore potential emigrants.

The only thing we know is that, paradoxically, urbanization makes the situation slightly better, because it partly reduces the enormous stress on the environment caused by the need to find land for the new inhabitants of the world. In the Middle Ages, colonization occurred precisely for this reason: if the population grew beyond a certain level, some people had to leave, cut down forests, and settle there. The colonization of Asia and, to some extent, of Europe was brought about by this subjugation of new territories to cultivation and therefore changing the environment. In countries like India, one of the few examples left in the world of an enormous population still largely dependent on agriculture, the effects can still be seen in terms of how few forests, uncultivated land, and wild animals have survived.

Today, things could go in another direction. Fortunately, if you take the world as a whole, urbanization provides us with a different solution, a place to settle the new arrivals without necessarily exploiting new tracts of land on a large scale. A more urgent problem is the bad population distribution around the globe. The unavoidable conclusion is that there will be massive pressures for emigration from the countries with very high birthrates to the rich countries. But, as we have seen, one of the principal features of the modern world is that immigration is increasingly curbed or obstructed in the rich countries. Yet to me it seems inevitable that, one way or another, the countries that don't reproduce their populations, like Italy, will import cheap labor or people who will do those jobs that the indigenous population no longer wants to do. It seems equally inevitable to me that this workforce will be imported from poor countries, and increasingly from the Third World. We have already seen migratory exchanges of this kind: the most common is the use of Filipinos as domestic servants. I recently read an interesting study on Salonika: it was once a multicultural city, inhabited by all the peoples of the Ottoman Empire. It was primarily a Jewish and Muslim city. A gradual process of ethnic cleansing throughout the twentieth century has turned it into a city that is 99 percent Greek. However, current migratory phenomena are changing it again, because the Greek middle classes are resorting to Filipino maids and Albanian gardeners on a massive scale. The same is occurring in California, with the only difference that the gardeners are Mexican. The demand for services that cannot be provided by the indigenous population, because of the scarcity of cheap labor, will undoubtedly lead to the transfer of many more people from the Third World to the First.

This will pose an enormous political and social problem, because Europe is a tendentially protectionist society that wishes to keep foreigners outside its borders, even if they are Kosovar refugees. The wealthy countries are increasingly reluctant to allow right of entry or citizenship to foreigners. The current situation of strong demand on the one hand and restrictive measures on the other runs the risk of creating two societies: the first enjoying full citizenship and rights, and the second made up of foreigners, displaying all the features of a permanent underclass. Some of them will obtain forms of citizenship, but the majority will in some ways be considered an inferior race, at least in terms of citizenship. Half the immigrants living in Europe are already doing so illegally, and in an underground manner. In practice, this means they have no rights. In the short term, the victims of this situation will not feel its full weight, because if you are an immigrant from black Africa, you are better off earning your living in Florence than you would be in your home country, even without the rights of a citizen. However, this process will create an apartheid society. Indeed, the true characteristic of apartheid is not the separation of races, as most people think. In South Africa, the races mixed in all fields of their collective life, but some enjoyed rights that others were barred from.

As long as immigrants are a relatively small minority, there may not be any serious political problem. But today, this is no longer the case. In Germany and Austria, foreigners are already about 10 percent of the population. Europe's rigid restrictions on immigration will not be able to prevent a further percentage increase, which could create political tensions and serious moral dilemmas.

Then there is the risk of racism, which arises from the fact that the greatest immigration comes from the Third World. For some reason that I do not fully understand, but which has been demonstrated historically, it is more difficult for people with different features and a different color of skin to be accepted. I'm sure the great unresolved and unmentioned question of the European Union is to what extent it can be enlarged to include Muslim countries. This is why, in my opinion, Turkey has been left outside the door. Essentially, the trend toward Islamic fundamentalism in Middle Eastern and North African countries is a reaction against the racism of European countries. This complicates things further, and gives rise to powerful local tensions, as has already been experienced in France and Great Britain. The failure of the rich countries of Europe to reproduce their populations is not therefore solely a demographic question.

I wonder what will happen to the less affluent Eastern European countries that are displaying similar trends of population decline. I cannot say, but I'm sure this will produce large upheavals there too. The countries of ex-Yugoslavia and ex−Soviet Union will in fact be less populated than they were fifty years ago. This is not only because they have low birthrates, but also because their populations are being massively drained by emigration. Many leave out of choice; others are expelled, as in Bosnia and Kosovo, and tend not to return. It is possible, for instance, that there will be a tendency for Chinese and Koreans to cross their borders with Russia into what is increasingly an empty land: Siberia.

These countries will have even greater demographic problems, because they will not be capable of maintaining the necessary economic infrastructures for supporting larger populations. It cannot be ruled out that they will deal with the situation by attempting to invert the trend and encouraging higher birthrates. Equally, the stabilization of demographic growth, or failure to do so, will have significant effects on the economies of developing countries, because a country with a high birthrate has to allocate greater resources to supporting mothers, children, health, and schooling, and therefore has to divert them away from growth.

Then we should consider the collateral developments which, although perhaps less obvious, are no less significant. It is now clear that even where the population is falling, the demand for education is not falling as well. Primarily, this is because an increasing number of young people are tending to study longer, but it is also because older people and pensioners are also displaying greater interest in continuing education, a phenomenon that tends to be neglected. I believe that there is a large market for the rapidly expanding business of education for adults: special courses, universities for the third age, and permanent professional training that lasts for people's entire working life.

*Ten billion human beings in 2050 is the most optimistic forecast. It is the one we will achieve if the UN's birth control programs are successful around the world. But if those programs fail, there could be twelve billion, twice the current figure in the short span of half a century. Will the environment be able to withstand this enormous stress?*

I don't think that the most serious problem is producing enough food for everyone. In the last fifty years, the world has produced enough or more than enough food to keep pace with the tripling of the population. It has done this with relatively backward or not particularly modern technology, such as selective breeding rather than the use of biotechnologies which are now becoming available. I don't see why this production trend should not continue in the immediate future. Indeed, I would say that the amount of food in the world today could sustain a large increase in population. This is why I am not convinced by the arguments of the industries that produce genetically modified foods, according to whom this is the only way to feed the world. This is not the case, at least on the basis of current predictions for population growth. This does not mean I am against biotechnologies. I am simply saying that this is not a valid argument, because we are not on the threshold of a food shortage. With a few unfortunate exceptions, the majority of the people in the world are better fed today than they were before. There is also an immense waste of food in the world due to its uneven distribution.

There will be consequences for the environment and ecosystem, and they will be serious. For the first time in history, humanity is capable of exhausting the stock of some nonrenewable resources. For example, no one would have ever dreamed that we could have fished out the North Sea. Yet this is exactly what happened. Today, we are capable of making the world unlivable, because of poisons, pollution, or the way in which industry modifies the atmosphere. Awareness of this problem is recent. It didn't exist before the seventies, at least not on a global scale. Although there has been a deplorable tendency to discuss these themes in rather catastrophic terms, there can be no doubt that humanity's power to degrade the environment has become very dangerous. Naturally, the more there are of us, the more dangerous we will be.

No one worried about the future of nonrenewable sources of energy, like coal, before the mid-nineteenth century.

Equally, very few feared the exhaustion of petroleum reserves before the end of the Second World War. Today, we can be a little more relaxed, because we know that alternative resources have been discovered. But the fact remains that those old resources are not renewable. Once they have been completely used up, there will never be any more. Although it is unlikely that we will exhaust them in the coming decades, or even in the next century, the fact that one day they will end is now written in the book of history.

The reality is that we have already changed the environment. To judge what will happen in the future, we should therefore base ourselves on past experience and on how people have behaved up until now. Over the centuries, we have witnessed historical phenomena of tremendous importance; for example, the deforestation of the Mediterranean region, partly through the spread of agriculture. This has had irreversible effects on the Italian landscape. There are very few corners of Italy which have preserved the old forests like those still found on the Sila Mountains in Calabria. Environmental degradation is not therefore a new phenomenon, but in the past it was a regional one, and now it is global. Today, the rainforests are being cut down, and many argue that this will have much more generalized effects than the deforestation of the Mediterranean.

This all raises important questions. To what extent are these effects reversible? What room is left for conservation? Let us suppose the world has already been transformed by human intervention into something that can no longer be called natural. Let us suppose that what we now call nature is no longer nature, but a combination of climate, topography, the original environment, and the effects of the long history of human intervention. What will this semihuman and no longer natural environment be? What difference will it make when the world around us will seem like a garden rather than a virgin forest? Our landscapes are for the most part man-made. Everywhere in the developed world, and without doubt in Europe, the environment has been transformed until the twentieth century above all by agriculture. But in the future, we will have to consider the effects of urbanization in a landscape that is no longer cultivated. What will happen to the rural areas where the agriculture that has molded it for long periods is no longer necessary, because it is inefficient? We have good examples in those areas that have been freed from the requirements of cultivation. There is a tendency among the European middle class to shift to the countryside and establish new types of infrastructure. This is what has happened in Tuscany with the decline of its particular form of sharecropping called *mezzadria*. It is a problem, because in many parts of Europe it was the old forms of agriculture that protected the landscape. What will happen once they have gone? The land could return to scrubland, or perhaps to forest. We don't know what will happen. But what I want to emphasize is that in this case we are not defending nature, but only a nature produced by agriculture manipulated by human beings.

What will happen in that part of the world where there isn't a middle class that builds a second home? It may be that the environment simply empties, as occurs in a large part of the American Midwest. But an empty landscape could return to a complete wilderness after a century or two. There is a great debate over how to conserve the existing environment, which is mainly engaged in by the more educated sections of affluent societies. This does not mean that it shouldn't be taken seriously: protecting tigers or rhinoceroses, for example, could be scientifically significant. Perhaps the rhinoceroses would all have been exterminated, if it had been left up to the local populations in Africa. Very few tigers are left in Asia. However, one thing I feel we must resist in the twenty-first century is precisely this attempt at conservation by creating living museums and establishing special and symbolic areas of the world that are supposed to maintain their "natural" features.

There are clearly good economic reasons for this kind of development. There is tourism, for example. It can be explained to African peoples that it would be better not to kill the rhinoceroses and gorillas, because more money can be made with the tourists who come to photograph them. So people will try to turn certain parts of the world into gigantic theme parks. But can this really be done? Will it be done for certain races that otherwise would not survive, as well as for animals? I am not exaggerating, there was just such a debate in relation to the tribes in the Amazon Forest. The question of how the environment is to be managed is increasingly becoming a practical rather than a theoretical problem, something that requires specific answers.

But let us suppose that it is not possible to take a piece of the world and conserve it as it was. The history of America tells us that this is theoretically possible. It is a history worthy of note, because, in spite of having ruined their environment more than any other civilization, the Americans have also been pioneers in conservation policies based on national parks. But let us, as I say, suppose that it is not possible. Well, I believe that we must learn in the twenty-first century to see large parts of the world for what they are: semiartificial environments. For example, we are discovering that residential suburbs, those agglomerations of single-family houses with gardens that are so common in Britain and North America, are an environment well suited to wild animals. They are perhaps the best possible environment for birds. There are more birds in the suburbs of British cities than in agricultural areas where they are annihilated by fertilizers. We have to get it into our heads that changing the face of the earth does not necessarily lead to a complete disaster. The environment can be changed sideways and not just by drastic vertical shifts from good to bad.

Another aspect of these possibilities we are considering is very visible in Great Britain. What happens when industries die? Here again, we have seen the tendency to build museums: so-called industrial archaeology. More interesting are the attempts to restore the environments that the first industrialization modified. I think that it is becoming increasingly possible to rehabilitate large areas of the world that currently appear completely ruined by industry. Try going to South Wales, an area where there was a large concentration of mines, and where thirty or forty years ago there wasn't even a tree growing as a result of pollution. Well, if you visit Swansea Valley today, you would not recognize the area and would find it hard to believe that there was ever an industry that amassed hundreds of thousands of miners in unhealthy conditions. Today, it is a splendid rural landscape.

The possibility of managing the environment therefore exists. The problem is how. And here I return to one of the great questions of the twenty-first century: who is going to do it? Who will be the authority that plans it and carries it out? Such authorities exist at the local and national level, but not at the global one. The greatest environmental dangers are now on a global scale. It is certain that the results will not be great if we let the market decide. The Mediterranean is a clear example. There are two extreme cases that show how a marine environment can be ruined and how it can be saved. Many miles of Spanish coast were completely destroyed by uncontrolled economic development, while in Dalmatia, development of the tourist industry was carefully planned under Tito, so that the region's extraordinary beauty and its ability to attract large volumes of business could be maintained together, without producing disasters. If you look at the two sides of the Adriatic, Rimini on one side, and Dalmatia on the other, you would think that you were looking at two different worlds. How to guarantee harmony internationally? That is the question.

*In your opinion, isn't the reduction in births in Europe also the sign of a tragic lack of faith in the future and of supreme selfishness? Is there the risk of condemning countries like Italy to the gradual disappearance of Italians?*

I don't believe that Europeans are not having any more children because they lack a future. I believe rather that in the past women had lots of children because they couldn't even envisage living in another way. It was the Lord's will. If the birthrate demonstrates anything, it demonstrates a higher level of education and an even higher level of financial planning. There are two moments in life when individuals end up under severe financial pressure: the first is when they have small children, and the second is when they are old and don't have savings to keep them independent. Clearly, not having children is a considerable economic advantage. In the past, children could be thought of as an asset to the family budget as they started work as peasants or workers, often when they were still quite small. Today, children are not earning until they are twenty or even thirty years old. The more they are educated and professionally qualified, the longer they are a burden on the family. It is therefore primarily a financial decision made possible by birth control.

In the nineteenth century, the legal system that regulated property and inheritance played a large part in demography. The French birthrate slowed down because the Napoleonic Code required them to divide the land among their children, while British aristocrats had lots of children, because only the firstborn inherited and the property therefore remained intact in both size and value. As you can see, economic factors can be very important. But even more important today is women's awareness that they can choose alternative lifestyles, because there no longer is the single model of motherhood. It is obviously a great step forward, but it is also a step into the unknown.

*What about projected life expectancies in the next century? An Italian woman could expect to live until she is eighty, while a Ugandan man can only look forward to thirty-five years. Isn't this the greatest injustice of the future world?*

In my opinion, the difference between life expectancy in rich and poor countries will paradoxically be easier to bring down than the difference in opportunity within the same society, between upper and lower classes. Take the example of a poor country that has experienced massive economic expansion, such as South Korea, the most extraordinary and rapid example that I can think of. Well, the difference in life expectancy between Korea and Sweden has been drastically reduced compared with thirty years ago. What is still very evident in wealthy societies is that those who start life with an advantage can watch that advantage multiply exponentially during their lives. A great deal of research has demonstrated that the poor do not live as long as the rich and do not enjoy as much good health. I don't doubt the rich also have their problems, but their relative advantage in terms of life expectancy, for example, is beyond doubt. The tragedy of the ex−Soviet Union demonstrates this very well. There has been a dramatic fall in their life expectancies, because impoverishment drastically reduces the basis on which human beings can build their future.

# Conclusion
# Hopes for the Future

*This has been the century of the "common people." Who now represents these common people?*

At the beginning of the twentieth century, the peasant was a typical human being who lived off the land. But at the end of the twentieth century, this is no longer the case. We could have chosen a worker, a member of the working class that grew enormously during the century, and probably reached its peak in the third quarter of the century. But today, its size and influence are shrinking fast. What about an office worker, someone who works at a desk in front of a computer? He or she wouldn't do either. An office worker would be fine for Western Europe or the United States, but there are still vast areas of the world where this image would not mean very much.

If you insist on looking for a symbol for the twentieth century, I would suggest a mother with her children. The people who have most in common are mothers, wherever they live on the face of the earth, and in spite of their different cultures, civilizations, and languages. In some ways, a mother's experience reflects what has happened to a large part of humanity in the twentieth century. What is no longer typical in our era is the traditional family structure that develops around the mother. Of course, there wasn't only one type, but almost everywhere there was some family structure. This is no longer true today.

But in spite of the fact that humanity's variety and the rapidity with which it has changed during the twentieth century make it very difficult to choose a symbol for the "common people," if there has to be one, I would choose a mother with her children.

*You have been possessed by one of the great demons of the twentieth century: a passion for politics. You were a communist activist from distant 1936, throughout the events of the war and the postwar period up to 1956. After that, your political orientation did not change, but you became increasingly detached. Have you ever regretted your activism? Did you ever think that it clouded your intellectual freedom?*

I hope that it never restricted my intellectual freedom. However, I have to admit that any real and strong political or religious commitment tends to impose—I wouldn't say obligations—more a preference or a prejudice favorable to advancing the cause. You realize this when you are reluctant to criticize it, when you are reluctant to apply the same critical intelligence to it as you have used to judge other causes. A Catholic scholar is tendentially less enthusiastic about investigating the Holy Inquisition than an atheist or a Protestant. Similarly, it is clear that scholars who were critical of communism have less hesitation in studying phenomena like the gulags, while a communist historian would certainly prefer to avoid it. I therefore have to admit that, while I hope I have never written or said anything about the Soviet Union that I should feel guilty about, I have tended to avoid dealing with it directly, because I knew that if I had, I would have had to have written things that would have been difficult for a communist to say without affecting my political activity and the feelings of my comrades.

This is also why I chose to become a nineteenth-century historian rather than a twentieth-century one. I could see that what was coming out of the Soviet Communist Party in terms of contemporary history was not acceptable. Thus I didn't want to be involved in debates that would either have taken me over onto the other side, or have brought me into conflict with my conscience as an academic.

After 1956, my activism was transformed into something different and more detached. From that time, it was clear to me that the dream was over. The general secretary of the Communist Party of Great Britain, of which I remained a member almost up to the date of its dissolution, used to say in difficult moments that he could have done with a direct telephone line to Moscow. He thought the party was an army of messenger boys, while those who worked in intellectual professions realized that we had to try to think things through on our own.

In 1956, I told the party leaders that I fully intended to maintain my friendships with those who had been expelled, particularly E. P. Thompson and the other dissidents whom I sympathized with, and if it wasn't all right with them, they could throw me out. But I didn't want to leave at that time, because I didn't want to end up in the company of all those ex-communists who had become anticommunists.

Why did I stay for all those years after the 1956 crisis? I think out of loyalty to a great cause and to all those who had sacrificed their lives for it. When I became a communist in 1932, this was what we all were ready to do. I can remember all the friends and comrades who died for that cause, who suffered prison and torture by communist regimes as well as capitalist ones, and we should not forget the men and women who gave up the chance of a successful career to work incredibly long hours in relative poverty as party officials, paid a worker's salary. I never had to make such sacrifices. The least I could do was show a little solidarity by rejecting the material and career advantages that could be gained from leaving the Communist Party.

Besides, communism wasn't Russia. It was a global cause. One of my first political experiences, when I became a party member while still a student in Berlin, was an argument with a comrade responsible for my recruitment. I disconcerted him because I said, "Well, we know that Russia is a backward country, so we can expect communism in Russia to experience defeats." He clearly was not of this opinion, while I never ceased to believe it. Like many other communists, I never agreed with the terrible things that happened under that regime. But if you think that communism is something greater than the history of the backward countries in which it happened that communists got to power, then that history is not reason enough to abandon the chosen cause.

Do I regret it? No, I don't think so. I know very well that the cause that I embraced has proved not to work. Perhaps I shouldn't have chosen it. But, on the other hand, if people don't have any ideal of a better world, then they have lost something. If the only ideal for men and women is the pursuit of personal happiness through the attainment of material assets, then humanity is a diminished species.

I have always been struck by the character of Andrew Carnegie, the only American multimillionaire who was both an atheist and a political radical. He once said, "A multi-millionaire who dies a multi-millionaire has wasted his life." This means that there is something else of significance besides becoming rich and famous. This desire may or may not be inherent in human nature, but it was certainly a historical phenomenon from the eighteenth century onward, when humanity began to understand that there is a possibility of improving and emancipating the world.

The problem isn't wanting a better world; it is believing in the utopia of a perfect world. Liberal thinkers are right when they point out that one of the worst things about not only communism, but all the great causes, is that they are so great that they justify all sacrifices, whether imposed on oneself or on others. This liberal argument is valid when it claims that only those with moderate expectations of the world can avoid inflicting terrible evils and suffering on it. Yet I cannot help feeling that humanity couldn't function without great hopes and absolute passions, even when these experience defeat, and it becomes clear that human action cannot eliminate human unhappiness. The great revolutionary leaders were aware of the fact that certain aspects of human life were beyond their efforts; for example, that men are unhappy in love. But when you are sixteen years old, you can even believe in this.

If you look at the great causes in which people of my age have been involved, such as the war against Nazism, it is impossible to say that the price paid was higher than the results obtained. Would the world be better if we hadn't resisted? I don't believe that there is a single person involved in that battle that is willing today to say that it was not worthwhile. Even with hindsight, it is impossible not to recognize that we did a great deal of bad, but also a great deal of good.

The problem is not political commitment, but the nature of that commitment. Is it directed toward the great causes of the Enlightenment: reason, progress, and the betterment of the conditions of all human beings? Or toward other causes that can be just as strong emotionally, such as nationalism or racism? They are not the same thing. And I think that communism was part of that tradition of modern civilization that goes back to the Enlightenment, to the American and French revolutions. I cannot regret it. In any case, activists in countries like Italy or Great Britain cannot be held responsible for what happened in other countries, and certainly not in Russia. The most that I can say about us is that in some cases we knew or intuitively guessed things that we kept to ourselves. But anything we could have said would have had no effect in the Soviet Union.

*Are you in any way nostalgic about the century that is drawing to a close? Do you subscribe to Isaiah Berlin's comment, "I look back on the twentieth century as the most terrible century in Western history"? Or can something be salvaged?*

What Berlin said is true, but it is not the whole truth. From any point of view, it has been an extraordinary century. And not just for its catastrophes. Indeed, at its close, the world is better than it was, with a few exceptions. It is not right therefore to dismiss the twentieth century in toto, because the children of this century are in better condition both materially and spiritually than were their fathers and grandfathers.

The problem is what the future will be like. This is my worry. From a technological point of view, in the next century humankind will almost certainly continue to celebrate triumphs of genius, it will be economically better off, and will perhaps be able to adapt to its new environment and learn to use the enormous forces at its disposal without destroying itself or the conditions of life as we know it. Whether it will actually do this will depend on global political decisions and is another question. Earlier we discussed the absence of any authorities capable of taking such decisions, so I am not sanguine about the chances. Still, there is nothing like fear, magnified into panic by the self-propagating process of media frenzy, to speed up action, particularly in the USA, which has an effective veto in these matters. If global warming and the rising curve of hurricanes and floods produces a particularly scary combination of climatic catastrophes, this might—just might—one day do the trick.

Much more troubling, and not only for moral reasons, is the dramatic widening of social and economic inequalities, both within states and between regions and countries. It is tempting to neglect this within the rich countries on the grounds that it does not matter that the gap between the "seriously" rich and the rest is growing rapidly, so long as the poor (i.e., those with less than half the average national income) are also better off in material terms, and anyway, the "underclass" only amounts to a smallish minority of the population. I don't think we can or should neglect this. Can we really be satisfied with a situation within the USA in which the ratio of top corporate executives' to factory workers' pay widened by a factor of 10 in less than 20 years, and now (1998) stands at the extraordinary figure of 419:1? [*International Herald Tribune*, 6 September 1999]. Or indeed with one where, at the end of two decades of spectacular national enrichment, the poorest 20 percent of Americans is getting 9 percent less income (after inflation) than it did in 1977?

Still, be that as it may, we cannot overlook the extraordinary increase of the global gap between the rich and the poor in the era of free-market fundamentalism. By one calculation, the top 20 percent of the world's population enjoys an income 150 times as high as that of the bottom 20 percent [*International Herald Tribune*, 2 February 1999, p. 6]—and the gap continues to grow. Patently,

> "A billion people living in dire poverty alongside a billion in widening splendor on a planet growing ever smaller and more integrated is not a sustainable scenario."

It is not sustainable even if the absolute situation of the bottom billion is improving a little, especially in an era of headlong change and a strikingly unstable and unpredictable world situation. Indeed, this would mean that the poor of the world are better able to consider their position and to take action, rather than spend all their time and strength keeping body and soul together for another day.

What is more, a polarization of wealth puts an especially hard squeeze on the middle strata of the population, on whose modest contentment the political and social status quo in capitalist countries has always relied. Especially when they face not quiet growth, but the economic earthquakes which an uncontrolled global free market generates. Since in the 1990s the economic Richter scale has recorded only modest tremors in North America and the European Union, we tend to underestimate the potential impact of such upheavals. When did the American or European market for automobiles last fall by 40 percent in two years, as the Brazilian auto market has since 1997? (*Frankfurter Allgemeine*, 20 September 1999, p. 24) Before the 1997−9 slump,

6 percent of the readers of a South Korean newspaper considered themselves "upper class," 70 percent "middle class" and 24 percent in the "low income bracket"; in June 1999 the corresponding figures were 1 percent, 46 percent, and 53 percent. But then, almost half of those interviewed in this poll said that their income had decreased by more than one-third since the beginning of the slump.

The danger of this growing polarization is that, as the world is integrated in one way by globalization, it is increasingly divided in another way into a permanently inferior majority of states and a privileged and self-satisfied minority of states. This minority enjoys a self-reinforcing superiority of wealth, technology, and power (including military power), and such superiority and complacency are just as likely to be resented now as they were in the old days of imperial supremacies—perhaps more likely, since today's greater availability of information can more easily reveal the discrepancies. Even today these two factions of humanity can neither understand nor communicate with each other. During the NATO war against Serbia I shocked an Italian interviewer by stating the obvious, namely that the debate on the legitimacy of this war, however burning and justified, was

"not a global debate but an old-style eurocentric, or better, North Atlantic issue. . . . For the greater part of the world, including its intellectuals . . . this issue is beside the main point, which for most of them, is that it is an imperial operation of the West in the Balkans. . . . They are not concerned with the question of whether it is a just war and how it can be justified. . . . The question is not important for Chinese, Indian, or Latin American intellectuals, simply because they do not believe it is a new kind of war." (G. Bosetti ed. *L'ultima crociata? Ragioni e torti di una guerra giusta*, Rome 1999, p. 59)

In much the same way, observers in the Third World found it almost inconceivable that the bombing of the Chinese embassy in Belgrade was not an assertion of global hegemony, but an example—though admittedly a spectacular one—of military-bureaucratic incompetence.

Essentially the two worlds are talking past each other, because when they meet, what the poor world can see in the rich world is overwhelmingly, perhaps exclusively, its superiority: the assertion, in its own interest, of wealth, technology, and power. I have little doubt that this is the way the United Nations intervention in East Timor looks to most people in South and East Asia who pay attention to it, even though the case for it—unlike that in Kosovo—is convincing using the criteria accepted in the region.

And conversely, we are constantly confronted by Western ideologists—Mr. Fukuyama, the Doctor Pangloss of the 1990s, comes to mind—for whom the rich world's superiority simply expresses its discovery of the best of all possible designs for arranging human affairs, as demonstrated by its historic triumph. In simpler words, these ideologists have the conviction that Westerners know better—which is far from self-evident. As the tragic record of Western economic advisers in post-Soviet Russia shows, it may be difficult for intelligent and well-intentioned academics and consultants even to grasp what is happening in environments so different from their own, and shaped by such different histories and cultures.

Indeed, in a world filled with such inequalities, to live in the favored regions is to be virtually cut off from the experience, let alone the reactions, of people outside those regions. It takes an enormous effort of the imagination, as well as a great deal of knowledge, to break out of our comfortable, protected, and self-absorbed enclaves and enter an uncomfortable and unprotected larger world inhabited by the majority of the human species. We are cut off from this world even if the sum total of amassed information is everywhere accessible at the click of a mouse, if images of the remotest parts of the globe reach us at all times of day and night, if more of us travel between civilizations than ever before. This is the paradox of a globalized twenty-first century.

However, there is another aspect of the future that I cannot foresee with any clarity: that of political and cultural relations.

A great many of the solutions and structures that we had in the past have been destroyed by the extraordinary dynamism of the economy in which we live. This is throwing an increasing number of men and women into a situation in which they cannot appeal to clear norms, perspectives, and common values, in which they do not know what to do with their own individual and collective existence.

This is true of institutions like the family, but also of political institutions that were the foundations of civilization, what Habermas called "the public sphere." Politics, parties, newspapers, organizations, representative assemblies, and states: none of these operates in the way they used to and in which we supposed they would go on operating for a long time to come. Their future is obscure. This is why, at the end of the century, I cannot look to the future with great optimism.

# Index

# THE AGE OF REVOLUTION

## 1789–1848

### *Eric Hobsbawm*

*'Brilliant, powerful, fascinating'*
GUARDIAN

Eric Hobsbawm traces with brilliant analytical clarity the transformation brought about in every sphere of European life by the Dual Revolution – the 1789 French Revolution and the Industrial Revolution that originated in Britain. This enthralling and original account highlights the significant sixty years when industrial capitalism established itself in Western Europe and when Europe established the domination over the rest of the world it was to hold for a century.

*'A brilliant account of Europe in its revolutionary age . . . No one could ask for more'*
A. J. P. Taylor

*'The work is challenging, learned, brilliant in its analytical power, wide ranging in its lucid exposition of literary, aesthetic and scientific achievements and packed with novel insight'*
ENGLISH HISTORICAL REVIEW

*'Brilliant'*
TIMES LITERARY SUPPLEMENT

Abacus
0 349 10484 0

# THE AGE OF CAPITAL
## 1848–1875

### *Eric Hobsbawm*

Abacus
0 349 10480 8

# THE AGE OF EMPIRE
## 1875–1914

## *Eric Hobsbawm*

'Excellently and wittily written . . . a classic'
OBSERVER

The splendid finale to Eric Hobsbawm's study of the nineteenth century, *The Age of Empire* covers the era of western imperialism and examines the forces that swept the world to the outbreak of World War I – and shaped modern society.

*'A superb achievement, incisive, illuminating and readable'*
SUNDAY TIMES

*'Magnificent'*
GUARDIAN

*'A superbly rich and erudite portrait of a society which was evolving rapidly under a variety of pressures – economic, technological and political'*
TLS

*'It takes far greater gifts – and far greater nerve – to simplify and to scintillate than to criticise and to complicate. This outstanding book displays both these admirable qualities in abundance. As in the previous volumes, the prodigious learning is lightly and lucidly borne, the range of example and breadth of allusion could not be bettered, and the illustrations have been admirably selected in order to complement the text'*
NEW SOCIETY

Abacus
0 349 10598 7

# AGE OF EXTREMES
## The Short Twentieth Century
### 1914–1991

## *Eric Hobsbawm*

*'A masterpiece'*
GUARDIAN

*Age of Extremes* is eminent historian Eric Hobsbawm's personal vision of the twentieth century. Remarkable in its scope, and breathtaking in its depth of knowledge, this immensely rewarding book reviews the uniquely destructive and creative nature of this most troubled century, and makes challenging predictions for the next.

*'The power of Hobsbawm's exploration of the age of hot and cold wars lies in its brilliant synthesis of familiar, though sometimes forgotten, facts and ideas. It combines an Olympian, multi-lingual erudition and an addictively readable style'*
Ben Pimlott, INDEPENDENT ON SUNDAY Books of the Year

*'Quite simply the best book of the year'*
Richard Gott, THE GUARDIAN

*'The best account of our calamitous century . . . A marvellously imaginative set of essays on the period from 1914 to the collapse of Communism. For Hobsbawm, this constitutes virtually the history of his own life-time and ideas; and he draws the threads together with subtlety, compassion and a gentle, quizzical wit'*
John Simpson, SPECTATOR Books of the Year

*'A brilliant and stimulating book'*
Lord Blake, THE FINANCIAL TIMES

*'A magnificent piece of historical exposition . . . an essential read . . . Hobsbawm is a master historian and his version of events is thrilling'*
Bryan Appleyard, THE INDEPENDENT

*'It is a chastening thought that this book itself, with its staggering erudition, lucid prose and sanity of vision, may bear witness to a world which a brash postmodern culture is already in the process of burying'*
Terry Eagleton, THE SUNDAY TIMES

Abacus
0 349 10671 1

# REVOLUTIONARIES

## *Eric Hobsbawm*

Distinguished historian Professor Hobsbawm has devoted a lifetime's research to the concept and practice of revolution as a means for social change. Presenting a clear exposition of revolutionary ideals, this important collection of essays covers all aspects of revolution, such as the nature of anarchism, the history of communism, the influence of Marx and Lenin, guerrilla warfare and class struggle. Written with masterful assurance, Eric Hobsbawm's essays are crucial for a true understanding of twentieth-century history.

Abacus
0 349 11225 8